EXECUTED

Tom Williams
and the IRA

EXECUTED

Tom Williams
and the IRA

Jim McVeigh

First published in 1999
by
Beyond the Pale
BTP Publications Ltd
Unit 2.1.2 Conway Mill
5-7 Conway Street
Belfast BT13 2DE
Tel: +44 (0)2890 438630
Fax: +44 (0)2890 439707
E-mail: office@btpale.ie
Internet site: http://www.btpale.ie

British Library Cataloguing-in-Publication Data.
A catalogue record for this book is available from the British Library.

ISBN 1-900960-05-2

Printed by
Colour Books Ltd, Dublin.

For my mother and father, Rosaleen and Fonzy

R.I.P.

BRAVE TOM WILLIAMS

Time goes by and years roll onward,
Still a memory I shall keep
Of a night in Belfast prison
Unashamedly, I saw men weep.

For the time was fast approaching,
A lad lay sentenced for to die,
And on the second of September
He goes to meet his God on high.

To the scaffold now he's marching
With head erect he shows no fear
And proudly standing on that scaffold
Ireland's cross he holds so dear

Now the cruel blow has fallen,
For Ireland he has given all,
He, who in the flower of manhood
Proudly answered to her call.

Brave Tom Williams we salute you,
And never shall forget
Those who planned your brutal murder,
We vow we'll make them all regret.

Here's a word you Irish soldiers;
If on this path you chance to stray,
Keep in memory of that morn
When Ireland's cross was proudly borne
By a lad who lies within a prison grave.

THE BALLAD OF TOM WILLIAMS
(Air : *The Patriot Grave*)

One bright Easter Sunday e'er noontime had passed
On the Kashmir Road in the town of Belfast,
Six young Irish Rebels set out to proclaim
That the Spirit of Freedom still burned like a flame.

A gun battle followed, a constable died,
The young men were captured, imprisoned and tried,
They faced their accusers with heads proudly high,
For the killing of one man the six were to die.

When the world cried in protest, a plan was conceived,
The leader must die, but the rest were reprieved,
For the crown sought revenge and the news became known,
Tom Williams must walk to the scaffold alone.

Tom Williams, the leader, just barely nineteen,
A martyr for Ireland, White, Orange and Green,
When the men who condemned him are vanished and gone,
The name of Tom Williams will ever live on.

My name is Tom Williams, from Clonard I hail,
And tomorrow they hang me in Crumlin Road Jail,
Tho' my life may be ended tomorrow at dawn,
The cause that I die for, forever lives on.

So remember Tom Williams, remember with pride
And cherish the cause he fought for and died,
Let Freedom for Ireland be ever your goal,
Yes, remember Tom Williams and pray for his soul.

Contents

Acknowledgements   xvii

Foreword   xix

1. Beginnings   1

2. Easter Sunday 1942 – The Operation   21

3. Crumlin Road Jail: Trial and Appeal   33

4. The Reprieve Campaign   63

5. September 2nd – The Execution   79

6. 'Carry on My Gallant and Brave Comrades'   91

7. Resonances   99

8. Laying to Rest   103

Appendix : Instructions for Executioners   109

Footnotes and Sources   117

Acknowledgements

I wish to express my sincere thanks to all those who helped and encouraged me in the writing of this short book. Especially, Leo Wilson, Kate Campbell (RIP), Annie Caldwell, Mary Murray, Joe Cahill, Madge McConville, Alfie Hannaway, Toby McMahon, Jenny Meegan, Catriona Ruane, Tony Curry, Gerry Adams, my friends Kieran and Leila McMullan, Micheal Liggett and Glenravel Publications, Liam Shannon, POWs Padraic Wilson, Pat Magee, Noel McHugh, Philip Manning, Ta McWilliams, Tommy Quigley, and all those in the Sinn Féin POW Department, Mary, Leo and Seando. Many thanks to Joe Graham and his excellent publication 'The Rushlight Magazine' for providing some of the inspiration and background information, including some of the photographs, for this book. I would like to thank Paul Cooper and Mary McConville for their very generous offers of financial assistance and a special thanks to all those at Beyond the Pale Publications for seeing something of value in this work. Last but certainly not least I would like to thank my wife Martine for her constant support, always.

Jim McVeigh
Long Kesh
May 1999

Foreword

I n recent years we have seen a renewed focus on the life of Tom Williams as his friends, comrades and family sought to have his remains moved from Crumlin Road Jail and interred at the republican plot in Milltown Cemetery. I was proud to be part of that campaign to see Tom buried with dignity and respect.

In spite of the fact that little has been written about Tom Williams, he is still ranked amongst the greatest of our heroes. I have been amazed that, as I travelled throughout Ireland and abroad, wherever there is a gathering of Irish people, one of those that is always mentioned is Tom Williams.

I had the great privilege of being a friend of Tom Williams and although he was just nineteen years of age when he was hanged on 2nd September 1942, he was already a man of great determination, courage and bravery.

Following our arrest in Easter 1942 myself, Tom and four other volunteers were charged with murder and sentenced to death. Three days before the date of execution the death sentence on five of us was commuted to life imprisonment. The day we were informed of this decision was the saddest day of my life. It was the day too that I witnessed the great bravery of Tom Williams when he consoled us and said,

'Grieve not for me, this is how I wanted it from the start'.

If Tom was still with us today what would he say? I have no doubt it would be the same message he sent out from his prison cell a few days before his death, when he wrote, 'The road to freedom is paved with suffering, hardships and torture, carry on my gallant and brave comrades until that certain day'. How true were those words. It has been long. It has been tortuous. It is not completed yet. There is a lot of work to be done to bring about that certain day.

This book is an important contribution to our understanding of the life of Tom Williams. However, the importance of books such as this is not only in remembering the sacrifices of the past but also in ensuring that the ideal for which men and women such as Tom Williams died becomes a reality.

Sinn Féin want a free and united Ireland. Republicans of today oppose a partitioned Ireland just as Tom Williams opposed it. Partition has failed. Fifty six years on from Tom's death the vision of republicans remains vibrant and viable. The foundations of a new Ireland have been laid throughout Ireland from Kerry to Derry and Wexford to Antrim, built on the commitment and dedication of republicans such as Tom Williams.

I am proud to have been asked to contribute to this book, something which will keep the memory of Tom Williams alive in the minds of future generations.

Tiocfaidh ár lá.

Joe Cahill
March 1999

1

Beginnings

Thomas Joseph Williams was born in number 6 Amcomri Street in the Beechmount area of Belfast on the 12th May 1923. This was a year of pogroms. The civil rights lawyer and historian Michael Farrell notes that from the inception of partition:

> ...the unionists set about constructing an Orange and Protestant state with almost all political power and patronage in their own hands – right down to the humblest rural council – and operated an elaborate and comprehensive system of discrimination in housing and jobs which kept the minority in a position of permanent and hopeless inferiority.[1]

Through 1920, 1921, 1922 and into 1923, small Catholic enclaves right across Belfast came under vicious attack from rampaging Orange mobs, sometimes with the support of the new forces of the state. Loyalist murder gangs, many of them made up of members of the RUC and the Specials, waged a

vicious campaign of assassination against the Catholic
population. As well as the establishment of the RUC, the
authorities in the new northern state, with the approval of the
British cabinet, had sanctioned the setting up of a Special
Constabulary, in reality a sectarian paramilitary force. By the
summer of 1922 the RUC and the Specials had grown into a
heavily armed loyalist paramilitary force of around 50,000
predominantly Protestant males. *The Manchester Guardian*
in 1921 aptly described the role of this new force:

> The Unionists have an important ally, they have a
> coercive police force of their own…They [the
> Specials] have become what everybody who knows
> Ulster perceived they would become – the
> instruments of a religious tyranny …some of them,
> A Class, became regular RIC, the rest, the B and C
> classes parade their districts at night with arms,
> harassing, threatening, beating and occasionally
> killing their Catholic neighbours and burning their
> homes.[2]

Before moving to Beechmount, Tom's family had fled the
small Catholic enclave in the Shore Road area of Belfast after
their house was attacked and burnt. This small area lay beside
the York Street mill, which like others across Belfast provided
the staple employment for many working class families.
Because of its vulnerability this small community saw some
of the worst atrocities of the period. Perhaps the most notorious
of these incidents occurred in February 1922 when loyalists
threw a bomb into a group of Catholic children playing in
Weaver Street, killing a number of them and grievously injuring

many more. Dr McRory, the Catholic Bishop of Down and Connor at the time protested at 'the butchery of my people'. The death toll for that month alone, that included both Catholics and Protestants, was put at forty-four. By the end of 1923 the worst of these attacks were over and an uneasy peace descended on Belfast. But according to Jonathan Bardon:

> The price in blood had been heavy: between July 1920 and July 1922 the death toll in the six counties was 557 – 303 Catholics, 172 Protestants and 82 members of the security forces. In Belfast, 236 people had been killed in the first months of 1922, more than in the widespread troubles in Germany in the same period. In Belfast there had been a vicious sectarian war at a time of political turmoil, and yet the statistics speak for themselves: Catholics formed only a quarter of the city's population but had suffered 257 civilian deaths out of 416 in a two year period. Catholic relief organisations estimated that in Belfast between 8,700 and 11,000 Catholics had been driven out of their jobs, that 23,000 Catholics had been forced out of their homes, and that about 500 Catholic owned businesses had been destroyed.[3]

With the end of the Civil War in 1923, the IRA in Belfast had been left in ruin. A majority of the IRA in the North had supported Michael Collins and The Treaty. In Belfast alone the new Free State government paid salaries to seventy-two full-time officers and men. Many of these went South to join the new Free State army. Seamus Woods, a Belfast Battalion Commander, was one of those, becoming an assistant to the Chief of Staff, Dick Mulcahy.[4] Others left the IRA disillusioned and in many cases broken hearted, by the betrayal of their former comrades. But from the ruins a dedicated few began the task of rebuilding the IRA. Many young men and women continued to join the IRA believing it was their only means of self defence, for them and for their families. According to Leo Wilson, a veteran Belfast republican:

> When Joe Mc Kelvey's body was being returned to Belfast for burial in Milltown it was accompanied by both former volunteers, as well as those who had remained with the army. Some agreed that there was a need for a re-organisation of the IRA in Belfast. Accordingly, a meeting was held in the small clubrooms in Marquis Street, which was just behind St Mary's in Chapel Lane. These rooms were used by various groups prior to the building of the Ard Scoil in Divis Street.
>
> Only a small number of dedicated men were at the meeting. A Battalion Staff was elected, plus representatives for the following areas, Falls, Ardoyne, Bone, Carrick Hill, North Queen Street, Green Castle, Markets, Ballymacarret. Slowly but surely new recruits joined...[5]

Tom's uncle Terry Williams had been jailed for helping to defend the tiny Catholic enclave in the Shore Road area from sectarian attack and from his earliest age Tom grew up hearing these stories of persecution and resistance. But this was more than folklore; discrimination and sectarian violence continued to be a daily reality for Catholics in the northern state.

Tom was the third child of a family of six. His brother Richard was the eldest, followed by Mary who died of meningitis at the age of three. Tom was next and then baby

Sheila, who died shortly after birth. Indeed Tom's mother Mary died shortly after giving birth to Sheila at the young age of twenty nine, leaving Tom in the care of his father Thomas. Life was hard and early death was commonplace, especially among children. In the nineteen twenties and thirties infant mortality rates in Ireland were very high, almost 7% of all births. Diseases like tuberculosis and pneumonia killed thousands of vulnerable men, women and children every year.[6] So Tom, who was still only a small toddler, and his brother Richard went to live with their Granny Fay at 46 Bombay Street in the Clonard area of Belfast. A great bond of love and affection was to develop between Tom and his granny and it was upon her knee and in this small district that he began to learn of the struggle for Irish independence.

This small maze of streets grew up around the mill factories, the Blackstaff, Milford, Ross's, Greeves's, as well as Clonard Print Works. The few families who owned the mills accumulated enormous fortunes by exploiting working class people who were desperate for employment. Hours were long, pay was bad and working conditions were abysmal for the 'mill slaves', as James Connolly once described them. Clonard House, still standing today at the corner of Oranmore Street and Clonard Street, was owned by the Kennedys. The Kennedys were local mill owners who had amassed part of their great wealth by turning out material for British army uniforms. Indeed the influence of the British army and its exploits throughout the British Empire is reflected in many of the street names throughout the district, Cawnpore Street,

Bombay Street, Kashmir Road.

Clonard House was eventually taken over by the Catholic Redemptorist Order, who went on to build the Clonard Monastery adjacent to it, to service the growing Catholic population in the area. It took three years and around £32,000, the bulk of which was donated by the working class people of Belfast, to build the beautiful building that stands there to this day. Like most Catholic enclaves, the Clonard area was no stranger to sectarian attacks, including the Monastery itself. In July 1920 Brother Michael Morgan was shot dead by a passing British military patrol as he walked along a corridor of the Monastery. That same day three other local Catholics were murdered, Joseph Giles, Alec McGoran and Thomas Robinson. Tom's Granny Fay was a devout Catholic who attended Clonard mass every day and under her influence Tom himself was to develop a strong religious faith and a great affection for the Monastery. The same affection is generally shared by the people of Clonard and beyond, even to this day.

As a child Tom did not enjoy good health. He had severe asthma and was often very seriously ill. On many occasions his Granny Fay nursed the young Tom back to good health. Perhaps because of this complaint, he was a small child of slim build and a pale complexion. His brother Richard was the complete opposite, a tall lad, very strong and robust. As he grew to his teens, though, he largely outgrew these attacks and developed a fondness for sports such as swimming, football and hurling. Despite this, he remained a slim and boyish figure, growing to only five foot six inches in height and weighing

Copy of Tom Williams' birth certificate

Record of Tom Williams' baptism

less than nine stone. With wavey brown hair and striking blue eyes he was a handsome lad.

While they were still young boys, Tom's father left him and Richard in the care of their Granny Fay and moved south to find employment where he joined the new Free State Army. He eventually remarried and it was Tom's uncle Charlie Fay who became a father figure to the two boys. Indeed the young boys spent a great deal of their time in Charlie's house in Amcomri Street and were very close to their young cousins. Both Tom and Richard spent much of their free time in the fields around and between Beechmount and Clonard, carrying on and on occasion making mischief. Tom's cousin Annie Caldwell remembers him as a fun loving but gentle lad. One rainy day as the boys were returning from Amcomri Street, they passed an old donkey tethered in an open field. Feeling sorry for the old creature the boys proudly led the donkey home to their granny's in Bombay Street hoping that they would be allowed to care for it. They were chased from the front of the house and the two disconsolate boys were forced to lead the poor donkey back to were they had found it. On another occasion the boys were sent to Kennedy's Bakery for bread for their granny and on the return journey they decided that they would have a little fun on the sloping fields of the 'Flush' area. Much to their delight they discovered that the bags holding the bread were ideal slides, capable of taking them down the hills at great speed. By the time they eventually arrived home, their granny discovered that there was nothing but crumbs left in the bags.

The two young brothers attended St Gall's Primary School in the shadow of Clonard Monastery. Like many children of their age they had part-time jobs after school and both Tom and Richard had an afternoon job in a mushroom farm located near the Bog Meadows on the Falls Road. They left school at an early age and sought full-time employment. For most working class Catholics, discrimination meant that employment opportunities were limited and Tom was only able to find work as a message boy and as a labourer. He worked for a period in Greeves' mill and even found work in the Docks area in the aircraft factory there. In the months before his arrest he worked in a printing firm. Almost everywhere he worked his sincere and friendly personality, as well as his willingness to work hard, endeared him to his workmates and his employers. These were qualities that would impress almost all who met him.

While times were generally hard, the late twenties and thirties were particularly so, for working class Protestant and Catholic alike. A world-wide recession was affecting even those traditionally strong industries such as shipbuilding, linen production, etc., and unemployment among Protestants had sharply increased:

> For half a century before the Great Depression, Belfast's shipbuilding industry had been a world leader. The 1930's were a bleak decade for the shipyards, with employment falling from 24,000 in 1923 to 8,000 by 1934. [7]

To deal with these high levels of unemployment, the

Stormont Government operated an 'Outdoor Relief Scheme' (ODR). This scheme allowed unemployed men, having passed a stringent and humiliating means test, three days' work in any week building or repairing roads. This road resurfacing scheme had begun in 1929 and according to James Dennison:

> The men didn't get paid; they got chits for groceries and that sort of thing and they worked on jobs in the various streets. They had a big stone crusher and they dug up the cobble stones, crushed the cobblestones down to size and mixed that with sand and cement. Then they concreted all the roadways. And some of the men were in a very bad way. I can remember one occasion they were doing round the front of our house in Posnett Street and my mother happened to go out to the door and this man was sitting on the footpath and two or three other men round him. So she wanted to know what was wrong and the foreman said that this man hadn't had food from the previous day. So my mother brought him in and made him a meal. Conditions were very, very bad.[8]

By 1931 those on the scheme were now being paid a cash sum but for their work they were paid an inadequate amount. Working class protests and demonstrations against these conditions were organised across Belfast that united discontented Protestants and Catholics. These culminated in the ODR strike and riots of October 1932. The protesters were met by vicious attacks by the RUC. Reminiscent of current RUC practice, even then the RUC attackers reserved their worst for Catholic areas. A glance at the hospital lists provided at the time show that of all those suffering from gunshot wounds the majority were from predominantly Catholic areas.[9] On 14th October significant increases in relief wages were announced and Tommy Geehan, one of the strike leaders, declared that, 'A glorious victory has been achieved'.[10]

This working class unity, though, was to prove temporary as conservative and reactionary elements stirred up fears of Papish plots, IRA infiltration, and Communist conspiracies, splitting the protesters. According to Harry White, an active IRA volunteer at the time, the IRA were loosely involved in the ODR protests but not in any significant or organised way. The ODR strikes were followed in the summer of 1935 by further widespread sectarian attacks and riots in Belfast:

> ...the climate changed completely after the troubles of June, July and August 1935, when the police and 'B' men were once again seen to be on the side of attacking loyalists. There was an increasing polarisation after that, and more and more young people felt that the IRA was their only guarantee of safety.[11]

These events had a radicalising impact on many young men and women, including we can surmise, on the young Tom. As soon as he was old enough, he joined Na Fianna Éireann, the republican scout organisation founded by Countess Markievicz in 1909, becoming a member of the Con Culbert slua in the Clonard area. Alfie Hannaway, a boyhood friend of Tom's and his OC in Na Fianna, remembers appointing Tom to the rank of Quarter Master for the Company. He took his role in Na Fianna very seriously and all who came to know him were struck by his dedication and maturity, even at this early age.

The C Company slua, which comprised over thirty boys from the district, spent much of their time drilling, in fitness activities, and on occasion scouting for the IRA. They were also given lectures in Irish history. Most of these activities took place in a little hall in Kane Street, just off Bombay Street. From their own money the boys were able to equip the hall with a boxing ring, PT equipment and some tables and chairs. It was during these years that he formed his great love for his country and his commitment to the IRA. He read avidly about Ireland's history and perhaps fatefully, he developed a fond admiration for Kevin Barry, a young IRA volunteer who had been hung by the British in Dublin during the Tan War. By this time Tom was developing into a quiet and thoughtful young man. His cousin Mary Murray, who was also born in Amcomri Street, remembers:

> Tom was a very quiet person, more a listener, but he did enjoy a joke and had a good sense of humour. I can remember how his eyes twinkled as he listened and struggled to control his laughter...[12]

As soon as he was of age Tom joined the IRA and at seventeen became a volunteer in C Company in the Clonard area were he lived. At the time, C Company's area of command ran the length of the lower Springfield Road, along the Falls Road from Beechmount to Conway Street, encompassing the streets in between. By the time Tom joined the IRA in 1940 it was already two years into its campaign and feeling the effects of arrests on both sides of the border.

Even before the campaign had begun, the IRA had suffered

a series of setbacks. Following a divisive Convention held in March 1934, the IRA lost some of its ablest leaders, as they left to form the left-wing Republican Congress. Later almost its entire northern leadership were arrested during the course of an IRA court-martial in Belfast in 1935. Despite these setbacks the IRA continued preparations for a new armed campaign. Following another divisive IRA Convention held in April 1938, Sean Russell was appointed Chief of Staff and under his leadership the stage was finally set for a renewal of conflict.

The campaign began disastrously when on 28th November, three volunteers, Jimmy Joe Reynolds, John Kelly and Charlie McCafferty, were killed in a premature explosion near Castlefinn in Co. Donegal. Three weeks later on the 22nd December, internment was introduced in the six counties. On 12th January 1939 an ultimatum was sent to Lord Halifax, the British foreign secretary, calling for a British withdrawal from Ireland. It began:

> I have the honour to inform you that the government of the Irish Republic, having as its first duty towards the people, the establishment and maintenance of peace and order, herewith demands the withdrawal of all British armed forces stationed in Ireland...
>
> The government of the Irish Republic believe that a period of four days is sufficient for your government to signify its intention in the matter of the military evacuation and for the issue of your declaration of abdication in respect of our country. Our government reserve the right of appropriate action without further notice if, on the expiration

of the period of grace these conditions remain unfulfilled.[13]

The British did not take the threat too seriously and four days later, on Monday 16th, two large bombs exploded in London, three in Manchester, one in Birmingham, and one in Alnwick. The campaign that had begun with attacks along the border now shifted to the heart of England.

During the campaign in England, a campaign strikingly similar in many respects to latter-day IRA campaigns, there were around two hundred mostly small explosions across England. On Saturday 25th June 1939, there were three large explosions at the Midland, Westminster and Lloyds Banks in London. Shortly afterwards heavily armed police guards appeared across London at key sites. Despite these initial successes, by the end of the year the frequency of the attacks began to taper off. The campaign in England appears to have been poorly funded and indeed poorly organised, despite the best efforts of many of those involved. Harry White recalls a humorous but telling story of how after arriving in England to join the campaign he met up with another volunteer, Albert Price. It was a roasting warm autumn afternoon and he was suprised to find Albert sweating heavily, wearing a thick woollen pullover. Albert replied to Harry's expression of suprise by saying, 'I can't help it, I've no shirt'. Albert had come over to England penniless to join the campaign on a half used ferry ticket, bought on the docks at Belfast for five shillings.[14]

Before the campaign had begun, Russell had met the Taoiseach, Eamon De Valera, hoping to secure his support for his plans or at least his neutrality. Both were refused and soon afterwards De Valera had passed in the Dáil a Treason Bill and then later an even tougher Offences Against the State Bill. These laws would later be used to devastating effect against his old comrades in the IRA. On 9th September 1939, a raid on 16 Rathmines Park in Dublin led to the arrest of Larry Grogan and Peadar O'Flaherty, two members of the GHQ Staff, as well as the capture of thousands of US dollars. Before long, state executions, both in the Free State and England, would follow.

Like most other young volunteers Tom was an enthusiastic supporter of this campaign and was probably ignorant of the growing difficulties the IRA leadership were facing. When Britain declared war on Germany on Sunday 3rd September 1939, many republicans, including the young Tom, believed that the war presented the IRA with an opportunity to strike while British forces were fighting elsewhere. England's difficulty could be Ireland's opportunity again. Looking back, it is difficult for many people today, including some republicans, to understand the Free State's position of neutrality during the Second World War, or indeed the IRA's willingness to seek military assistance from the Nazi regime. But as far as most republicans were concerned the situation was quite straight forward. Britain was occupying part of their country, Britain was the enemy. The words of a poem/song from the period sum up the attitude of most republicans to the war between Germany and Britain:

> Who is Ireland's enemy?
> Not Germany nor Spain,
> Not Russia, France or Austria,
> They forged for her no chain
> Nor quenched her hearths, nor razed their homes,
> Nor laid her altars low,
> Nor sent her sons to tramp the hills
> Amid the winter snow.[15]

Despite whatever military advantages the war presented for the IRA, the advent of European war created the worst possible political circumstances. The campaign lacked the enthusiastic support of the Irish population, while De Valera, preoccupied by the threat of invasion by either Britain or Germany, stepped up the repression of republicans.

While the IRA campaign in England lost momentum, Tom and his comrades spent much of their time gathering intelligence on RUC patrols and military installations. They also trained in the use of small arms or at least those that were available to the IRA, mostly a handful of revolvers, Lee Enfield rifles and even scarcer Thompson sub-machineguns. Scattered throughout the Clonard area were a considerable number of homes friendly to the IRA but Tom's local company also held some of their meetings, drills and weapons lectures in the basement of St Gall's School, where he had been taught as a boy. On one occasion Tom was almost shot when a handgun he was handling accidentally discharged, ricocheting noisily around the basement.

Because of his dedication and his remarkable ability Tom

was soon appointed Adjutant of C Company and in the months before his final arrest, at the young age of eighteen, he became the Officer Commanding. A Company normally comprised four or more Sections. In 1942 C Company had seven Sections with around ten volunteers in each Section. The Company staff consisted of an OC and Adjutant, both of whom held the ranks of First Lieutenant and Second Lieutenant respectively, a Quarter Master, an Intelligence Officer, a Finance Officer and a Training Officer. Of course the extent to which these roles and structures actually functioned varied greatly from Company to Company, and from period to period. Numbers fluctuated as arrests took their toll on already depleted ranks. Nonetheless, his appointment to the rank of Company OC was a considerable responsibility for one so young.

By all accounts he was a disciplined and demanding OC, yet fair with all those under his command. He himself was totally committed to his work within the IRA and expected others to be likewise. Madge McConville, nee Burns, one of those arrested with Tom, remembers him as a quiet young man who was always polite and respectful with people. Despite his natural tendency to shyness, he went out of his way to be friendly, especially when in the homes of IRA supporters. Madge recalls:

> He was a very quiet lad, very well liked, everybody liked Tom. He was the sort of fella who would've come into the house and had a yarn with anybody. Now our Willie was odd, you know how odd our Willie was. The rest of them would've run in past our Willie, looked at him and never bothered with

> him. But he would've talked to Willie and our
> Willie appreciated that. For that I got away with
> murder when Tom was about. I kept stuff in the
> house and anytime there was stuff in the house there
> was murder between me and Willie. When Tom
> was there, when the stuff was being taken out, there
> was never a word said. [16]

Meanwhile the war in Europe gathered momentum. The French coast from Belgium to Spain was now under German control. When the initial threat of a German invasion of Britain faded, Hitler turned his attention to strangling Britain, to sapping its will to fight. The strategic importance of the six counties to the British war effort became critical. Northern ports from Derry to Bangor became vital to keeping the Atlantic shipping lines open. Derry in particular became one of the largest Anglo-American naval bases in Europe. Harland and Wolff's capacity became vital to British wartime production. While German submarines wreaked havoc in the Atlantic, it was only a matter of time before German bombers would turn their attention to the North.

The IRA was strongly opposed to any Irish man or woman joining the British services to fight in the war against Germany but to provide cover for its activities, encouraged its members, including the young Tom, to join the Air Raid Patrol. So Tom became an air raid warden in the Clonard area. The first German attacks on the six counties came on the 7th and 8th April 1941. A small number of incendiary bombs were dropped over Belfast by six German bombers, a diversion for the more extensive attacks on Glasgow and the Clyde. But on the 15th and 16th that same month, over one hundred German bombers attacked Belfast with deadly consequences. Over seven hundred people were killed and thousands of others injured. That night Tom was one of those who led people, many of them Protestants from the Cupar Street/Shankill Road area, to safety in air raid shelters scattered about the district. Clonard monastery again provided sanctuary for local people, as they sheltered in the crypts below the church.

Like most young people in times of conflict, Tom and his friends also found time for fun. He often attended football matches and though quiet and reserved in his own way, he was an enthusiastic attender at céili's and rarely lacked a partner. Most young nationalists from across Belfast attended céili's in Pearse Hall or Banba Hall in King Street and another hall in Bread Street, in Belfast city centre. Even on occasions such as this, Tom's thoughts rarely strayed from the IRA. Joe Cahill recalls:

> ...even if you went to a céili or anything like that, he'd maybe turn around in the middle of a dance and say, 'I wonder how long this is going to last?' and he would be talking about the British occupation of Ireland.[17]

It was probably on one such occasion that Tom met his one serious girlfriend, Nell Morgan. They dated from an early age and by all accounts were very much in love. They had the occasional fallout over Tom's busy IRA schedule, but remained close for all that. Even during his time in Crumlin Road Jail, she continued to visit him regularly.

2

Easter Sunday 1942:
The Operation

The dramatic events that culminated in the execution of Tom Williams began on Easter Sunday 1942. Easter has an important place in the republican calendar and in 1942 Belfast republicans were determined to commemorate the 1916 Rising. The problem was that since the 1920s republican parades of any description had been banned, as had most labour demonstrations. In 1922 the Civil Authorities (Special Powers) Act had been passed by the new Stormont regime. This allowed the Minister for Home Affairs to prohibit any '…meetings, assemblies …or processions in public places'. The Minister was under no obligation at all to provide any justification, legal or otherwise, for the decision to ban any gathering. The Special Powers Act (as it became known) was regularly invoked over the years to ban republican parades and meetings, but rarely affected loyalist marches. Indeed the 12th of July was designated a bank holiday in the new state and remains one to this day. Sir Richard Dawson Bates, an extreme loyalist who had been closely associated with the formation of the UVF, was the Minister for Home Affairs in the Stormont regime, a post he held for an incredible twenty two years. He had this to say in the Stormont Parliament about his attitude towards parades:

> We are not going to tolerate disloyal meetings called in the name of politics with the object of bringing about the disruption of Northern Ireland.[18]

In 1931 two republicans were arrested after an Easter parade in Newry and sentenced to twelve months hard labour. When republican marchers did assemble, they were viciously assaulted by the RUC and Specials. The penalties for opposing these oppressive laws could be harsh.

It was decided by the IRA leadership in Belfast that three separate Easter parades would be held and that a number of diversionary operations would be carried out in other areas across Belfast. Tom, as the OC of C Company, was instructed by his Battalion staff to make the necessary preparations for an operation in the Clonard area. A volley of shots was to be fired over an RUC patrol car that regularly passed by the corner of Clonard Gardens and the Kashmir Road and the volunteers were to withdraw to safety.

In the days preceding the operation, Tom selected and briefed those volunteers who would take part: eight in total, including Tom himself. The youngest of the group, Margaret Nolan, was just sixteen years old, the oldest twenty one. They met on the day of the operation and at around 2.30pm, took up their allotted positions. Pat Simpson, along with two young women, Margaret Burns and Margaret Nolan, waited in Cawnpore Street to collect the weapons after the operation. Tom and his four other comrades, Joe Cahill, Jimmy Perry, 'Dixie' Cordner and John Oliver, took up positions on the Kashmir Road and waited for the RUC patrol to arrive. All five were armed with a variety of weapons, a short Webley revolver, three Webley revolvers and a semi-automatic Luger parabellum.

Shortly after 3pm, an RUC patrol car carrying four constables turned into Clonard Street and headed towards the junction of Clonard Gardens and the Kashmir Road. On board were Sgt Archibald Lappin, the driver, Constable George Williamson, Constables Patrick Murphy and David McMahon. All four were armed with their service revolvers; in addition McMahon carried a pump-action shotgun. As the Ford V Light car passed the junction into Clonard Gardens, Tom and his comrades opened fire over the car. For some reason, either deliberately or accidentally, we cannot now be sure, one of the bullets fired actually struck the car, smashing a rear window but missing any of the occupants. Constable Williamson accelerated into Clonard Gardens, where instead of hastily driving away, Lappin, McMahon and Murphy alighted, drew their weapons, and set off at a run back towards Cawnpore Street and the scene of the shooting. The stage was now set for a confrontation that would have far reaching and tragic consequences.

At this point in the IRA operation things started going disastrously wrong. According to Joe Cahill:

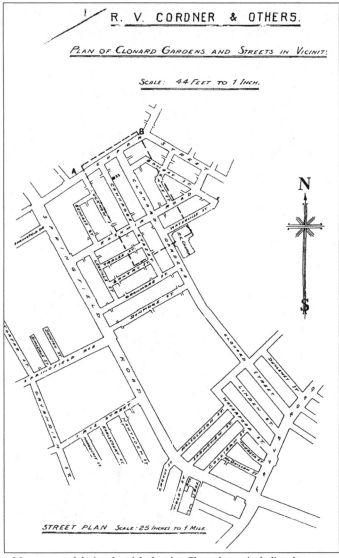

Map presented during the trial, showing Clonard area, including the scene
of attack on the RUC patrol

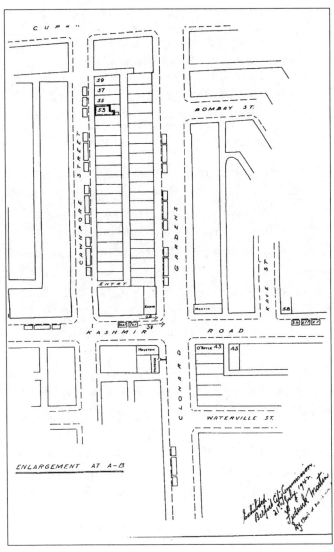

Detail of area showing Cawnpore Street where Constable Murphy was shot

> There seemed to be some confusion. Pat was there
> and we asked him where the rest where; he said
> they'd went down the entry. Now nobody was to
> go down the entry. We were to go in the opposite
> direction actually. The only people who were to go
> down the entry were the two girls and Pat Simpson,
> down to number 53. Tom said, 'We'd better go
> down and get them out of this house, get them to
> hell out. We'll go out the bottom end of the entry'.[19]

Instead of leaving the house immediately, all five were
offered, and rather foolishly accepted, minerals from the
woman of the house, a Mrs Mary O'Brien.

Meanwhile, Sgt Lappin, Constables McMahon and Murphy
raced into Cawnpore Street in hot pursuit. It was Murphy who
entered Cawnpore Street entry in time to see Pat Simpson and
Margaret Burns enter number 53 by the back door. He returned
to his colleagues in Cawnpore Street and told them that a
number of suspects had entered a house somewhere near the
bottom of the street. Lappin then directed Murphy to return to
the entry and cover the back of the houses, while he and
McMahon conducted a door by door search of the last few
houses.

As the last of the IRA group entered the back kitchen of
number 53, they alerted Tom and the rest of the group to the
presence of the RUC on their tail. They quickly re-armed
themselves and within seconds all hell broke loose in the tiny
back kitchen and scullery.

As they began their search of houses at the bottom of
Cawnpore Street, Lappin and McMahon sounded their police
whistles and in a few moments two other RUC men, Constables

Dougie Marshall and Robert Wilson joined them. Having found nothing suspicious in numbers 55, 57, and 59, Wilson, McMahon, and Marshall ran round into Clonard Gardens, while Lappin remained in Cawnpore Street. It was during these moments of confusion that Murphy made the brave but fatal decision to enter the backyard of number 53.

With his Webley revolver drawn (see photographs, exhibit 17) Murphy advanced across the small backyard towards the scullery of the house. He was spotted by one of the IRA group, who alerted the rest. In the controversial statement that Tom later made to the RUC while in hospital, he described what happened next:

> I ran into the scullery. There is a little glass enclosure in the yard and from the scullery window I could see a policeman coming into this enclosure with his gun drawn. When he was about three yards from me and beside the kitchen window, I pointed my revolver at his body and fired one shot. He staggered and fired back and I fired four or five more shots at his body.

At least two other weapons were fired. According to Joe Cahill, Jimmy Perry fired first through the kitchen window at Murphy and then probably Joe himself through the kitchen doorway. In the exchange of fire Murphy was shot five times, twice in the chest and three times in the stomach, with a sixth round striking his holster. According to the forensic evidence given at the trial, three of the rounds that struck Murphy were fired from a Webley revolver (see photographs, exhibit 6), the weapon fired by Tom, and two others from the short Webley (see photographs, exhibit 2). Before being fatally wounded in the heart, Murphy fired three rounds from his revolver, while a fourth misfired. All three rounds found their mark, striking Tom twice in his left thigh and once in his left forearm.

Mortally wounded, Murphy dropped to the floor of the scullery. Tom stepped over his body and stumbled towards the hallway of the house. He was able to tell his comrades that he had been shot, before fainting at the bottom of the stairs. Joe Cahill now took command of the group. Realising that the house was now surrounded by the RUC, they took refuge in the upstairs of the house. Tom, who was unconscious, was carried upstairs and laid on the bed in the back bedroom. Following a hasty discussion, the group decided that they would shoot it out with the RUC rather than surrender.

The three RUC men, Wilson, McMahon and Marshall, who had run into Clonard Gardens, were now joined by a Constable Allen. All four passed through a house in Clonard Gardens and into the back entry of Cawnpore Street. They noticed the back door of number 53 lying open. Cautiously, Allen and McMahon entered the back of 53 first, followed by Wilson and Marshall. It was Allen and McMahon who found Murphy lying dead in the small scullery. He lay face down, his head in the threshold of the kitchen, his revolver still clasped in his right hand. Wilson and Marshall proceeded forward into the hallway of the house, where they were met by Lappin and the woman of the house, Mrs Mary O'Brien. Lappin later recorded that while in Cawnpore Street, he heard a number of dull gun shots but was unable to tell where they were coming from. He

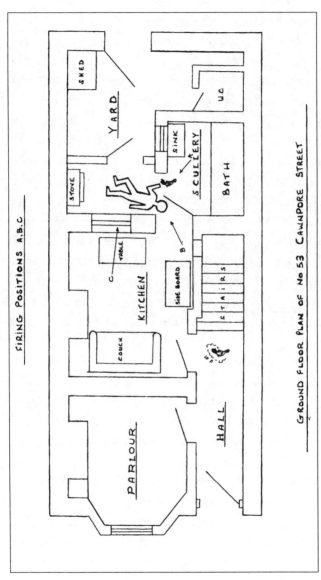

Drawing of the scene of the shooting of Constable Murphy, presented at the trial

then spotted a woman who appeared to be in a distressed state, standing at the front door of number 53. It was this that finally drew him to the scene of the shooting. On entering the hallway he saw a Webley revolver (see photographs, exhibit 6) lying in a pool of blood at the bottom of the stairs.

What happened next was the matter of some dispute at the subsequent trial. Joe Cahill went to go down the stairs and found a number of RUC men advancing up the stairs using the man of the house, a Mr Francis O'Brien, and his six year old granddaughter Mary Gilmore, as shields. Unable to fire for fear of wounding or killing the civilians, Joe retreated to the bedroom. By this time Tom had regained consciousness and on hearing just how hopeless the situation was, ordered the group to surrender. The four weapons (see photographs, exhibits 1, 2, 3 and 5) were placed on the dressing table before the first RUC men burst into the room. Having just viewed the body of their dead colleague downstairs the RUC men who entered the room were in a rage. Joe Cahill remembers one of them shouting: 'Who's this fucker lying here?' Joe replied that Tom had been shot. 'There's no reason why we couldn't shoot this bastard, they'd never know what Murphy shot him'. Joe threw himself across Tom's body, and said, 'Over my dead body'.[20]

Instead of shooting them, they proceeded to beat all of them mercilessly. The two young women, along with the householders, had been moved into the front parlour of the house. One of them recalled hearing shouts and loud bangs coming from the upstairs backroom. When later examined in

CORONER'S COURT.

(7 MA: 1)

City of Belfast. **Deposition of Witness** taken and acknowledged
TO WIT on behalf of our Sovereign Lord the King, touching the

death of Constable Patrick MURPHY.

at the Coroner's Court, Belfast, in the County

of Antrim, on day, the day of April

in the year of our Lord One Thousand Nine Hundred and 42 before me.

HERBERT P. LOWE, Medical Doctor, Coroner of our Sovereign Lord the King,

for the City of Belfast, on an Inquisition, then and there taken, on view of the

body of the said

as follows to wit:—

The Deposition of Sergt. Archibald LAPPIN

who being duly sworn upon his oath, saith

I am a Sergt. of the Royal Ulster Constabulary stationed at Springfield Road. I remember Sunday the 5th. day of April, 1942. about 3.20 p.m. on that date I was in charge of a patrol car which was being driven along Clonard Gardens towards Cupar Street. When passing over the intersection of Cashmir Road seven or eight shots were fired at the car. One bullet passed through the glass portion o the rear doors of the car from left to right. The driver stopped immediately and I got out, accompanied by the deceased and another Constable, and went in pursuit of three or four men whom I had seen shooting at us. We went along Kashmir Road and turned into Cawnpore Street. The deceased went into the entry at the rear of the houses and returned in a few seconds. As the result of what he told me I went to the third house from the Cuper Street end of Cawnpore Street and while there I heard shots. I later went into 53, Cawnpore Street and saw the deceased lying on his face in the doorway between the kitchen and the scullery. He appeared to be seriously injured.

Archibald Lappin

The Deposition of Sergt. Wm. J. Anderson who being duly sworn on his oath, saith

I am Station Sergeant at Springfield Road Barracks. I remember Sunday the 5th. April, 1942. About 3.35 p.m. on that date, as the result of information received, I went to 53, Cawnpore Street where I saw the deceased in the kitchen of the house. He appeared to be dead. The body was later conveyed to the Royal Victoria Hospital. ~~xxxxx~~

On the 6th. April, 1942 I attended a Post Mortem examination of the deceased at the Royal Victoria Hospital and identified the body as that of Constable Patrick Murphy. He was attached to Springfield Road Station and was 48.1/12 years of age.

J. Anderson

Depositions of Sergeants Archibald Lappin and William Anderson

custody, the five young IRA men arrested in the room with Tom were suffering from a range of injuries. Joe Cahill had the worst, a fractured skull, numerous broken ribs and extensive bruising. In evidence later submitted at trial, Head Constable William Heffernan described how having arrived at number 53 just after the shooting, he found Joe Cahill lying across the bed upstairs:

> Cahill was lying across a bed on the left facing inwards. His feet were outstretched over the bed. I asked him if he had been shot and he said, 'No, I was kicked in the ribs'. I got him on to his feet on the floor and found that he had what appeared to be a superficial wound on the right side of the head and an abrasion about one inch from the right eye, on the cheek. His face was smeared with blood.

He was covered in so much blood that he thought Cahill had in fact been shot.

It was another Head Constable, Murphy, who attempted to calm his hysterical officers down. Some of the RUC men present wanted to bring their captives to Springfield Road barracks, the barracks where the dead man had been stationed. Head Constable Murphy, realising the danger they would be in, refused and ordered that they be taken instead directly to Townhall Street RUC station.

3

Crumlin Road Jail:
Trial and Appeal

Following their arrest, all eight were eventually charged with Murphy's killing. The two young women were moved to Armagh Jail, while the men were taken to Crumlin Road Jail, except for Tom, who for the moment lay under armed guard in the Royal Victoria Hospital.

Still standing to this day, 'The Crum' as it was known to the many republicans who passed through its gates, remains remarkably unchanged. Modelled on the recently opened Pentonville Prison (1842), it was built around the middle of the nineteenth century opposite what was then the County Courthouse. For the prisoner, if not for the warder, it was a bleak and oppressive place.

One entered the jail from the Crumlin Road through its large front gates and into what became known in later years as 'The Circle'. This was a central administrative building that housed the governor's quarters, the reception area where prisoners

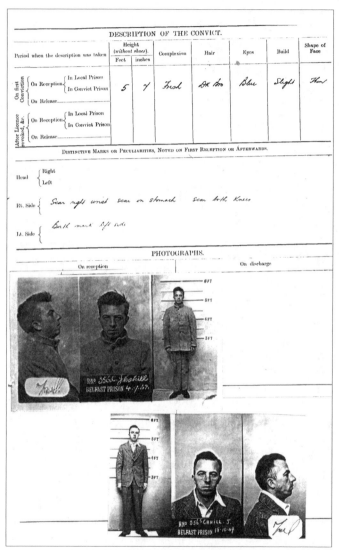

DESCRIPTION OF THE CONVICT.							
Period when the description was taken	Height (without shoes).		Complexion	Hair	Eyes	Build	Shape of Face
	Feet	inches					
On first Conviction — On Reception { In Local Prison / In Convict Prison	5	7	Fresh	Dk Bro	Blue	Slight	Thin
On Release							
After Licence revoked, &c. — On Reception { In Local Prison / In Convict Prison							
On Release							

DISTINCTIVE MARKS OR PECULIARITIES, NOTED ON FIRST RECEPTION OR AFTERWARDS.

Head { Right / Left

Rt. Side { Scar right wrist   scar on stomach   Scar both Knees

Lt. Side { Birth mark left side

PHOTOGRAPHS.

On reception — On discharge

RNo 3562. J. Cahill
BELFAST PRISON 4. 7. 47.

RNo 3565 CAHILL. J.
BELFAST PRISON 18. 10. 49.

A page from Joe Cahill's prison file, including
reception and discharge photographs

were processed, the officers mess and the chapel. From 'the circle' four long buildings radiated out in a semicircle shape like the spokes on a wheel. The first and last of these 'wings' A and D, faced onto the Crumlin Road, with B and C behind and between these two and hidden from sight (see photographs). Each wing was a three storey building that could house hundreds of prisoners in the rows of cells on each landing that looked down into an open well.

On arrival in reception, Tom's five comrades were photographed and given blue remand uniforms to wear. As remand prisoners charged with murder they were held on the bottom landing in C wing and kept in general isolation from the rest of the jail. There were a number of other republican prisoners in the jail but they were allowed no contact. The five now under Joe's command, slipped into the jail routine and within days were discussing ways and means of escaping. Incredibly within a few short weeks their opportunity would come.

In order to increase their opportunities to escape the five had offered to work in the wood yard in the jail. On a Saturday morning the wood yard was routinely cleared up and the five were detailed to do this. Any rubbish was gathered up and placed on the back of a small cart and brought to the back of the gardens to be dumped beside the outer wall. Much to their suprise, they were escorted only part of the way by one warder. Out of sight of any guards they tipped the cart up on its side and placed it against the outer wall. Joe Cahill was able to climb along the shaft of the cart and onto the top of the wall.

Below him was freedom. Joe hastily climbed back down and the five had a quick discussion about whether to escape there and then or wait until another occasion. At the time they believed it would be only a matter of days before Tom would arrive on the wing from the hospital and so, thinking of their comrade, they decided that they would wait and escape when all six could do so. Unfortunately a senior warder discovered that the five had been allowed to get close to the outer wall and their movement was immediately restricted within the jail. The opportunity to escape had been missed and would not come again.

Soon after this incident Tom was discharged from the jail hospital and joined his comrades on the Wing. Joe Cahill recalls that on their first meeting, Tom appeared to be 'stand-offish'. Sensing that something was wrong he spoke to Tom alone. Upset, Tom explained that he had broken an IRA order and had made and signed a statement to the RUC. Tom said that while lying injured, he had been told by a doctor and by members of the RUC that he was dying from loss of blood. Then, as now, the IRA ordered its captured volunteers not to co-operate in any way with the enemy authorities. Despite this, Tom, decided to make a statement accepting sole responsibility for the killing in the hope that it would save the lives of his comrades:

> I remember Saturday 4th April, 1942, I met James Perry, Harry Cordner, Joseph Cahill and John Oliver by appointment at precisely nine o'clock pm at a place which I do not wish to name. I

suggested that it would be a good plan to fire on the police patrol car as a protest against the English occupying Ireland. We arranged to meet at half past two pm the following day, Sunday 5th April, 1942 at a place which I do not wish to name. I armed all the party and myself with revolvers, one of which was a short Webley, three were Webleys and one was a parabellum. We then proceeded to the Kashmir Road vicinity where police car patrols are very regular and we knew that we would see a car soon. We were standing separately at two corners, two at one and three at the other. The car was then seen coming up Clonard Street towards Cupar Street and we ran into an Air Raid Shelter on the Kashmir Road and when the car approached the junction of the Kashmir Road and Clonard Gardens we all as I had previously instructed fired at the police car. I had instructed all the other four men mentioned to fire three shots each but I fired only one. There were about seven shots in all fired at the car. I had previously arranged that we should run into Cawnpore Street entry on the right hand side from Kashmir Road and to hand our guns to three persons who would be waiting there to receive them, (two of them were girls) after the shooting at the police car had taken place on the Kashmir Road. We did run into this entry and saw the three persons as arranged and as we ran past we handed the revolvers to them. They were to take the guns away and dump them elsewhere but it seems that the girls for some reason ran down the entry as someone shouted that the patrol car was at the bottom and that a policeman was coming down the entry and someone else shouted that the policeman had seen him coming into the house which we ran into. This was one of the men who was in our party. I ran into the parlour and I heard the police knocking the next door, the second one from Cupar Street. I then grabbed my revolver from the brown leather bag which was lying on the floor in the kitchen. This was the bag we put the revolvers into in the entry and was brought to the house by the girls. Someone of the eight persons (six men and two girls) said that a policeman was coming into the house by the entry door. I ran into the scullery. There is a little glass enclosure in the yard and from the scullery window I could see a policeman coming into this enclosure with his gun drawn. When he was about three yards from me and beside the kitchen window I pointed my revolver at his body and fired one shot, he staggered and fired back and I fired four or five more shots at his body. The revolver I had was reloaded by me after it had been brought to the house by the girls. No other person in the house had fired at Constable Murphy. I then shouted that I had been shot. I dropped my revolver and heard Constable Murphy groan and fall to the ground. Constable Murphy's body was lying between the glass enclosure and the door which leads from the scullery to the kitchen. I stepped over his body and ran into the hall of the house and there I fainted. Next thing I remember when I woke up on a bed in the back room up the stairs. Some of the party I had commanded said, "what do you want us to do?" I said, "where are the police" and someone answered, "they have the house surrounded" and I told them to surrender which they did. About five policemen came into the room where I was lying and they arrested us.

Sgd. Thomas Joseph Williams.

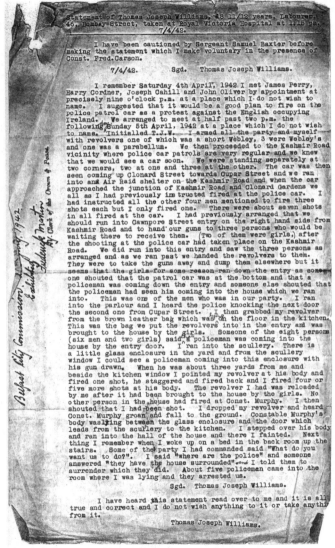

Statement of Thomas Joseph Williams, 18 11/12 years, Labourer, 46, Bombay Street, taken at Royal Victoria Hospital at 1.15 p.m. 7/4/42.

I have been cautioned by Sergeant Samuel Baxter before making the statement which I make voluntary in the presence of Const. Fred.Carson.

7/4/42.   Sgd.   Thomas Joseph Williams.

I remember Saturday 4th April, 1942.I met James Perry, Harry Cordner, Joseph Cahill and John Oliver by appointment at precisely nine o'clock p.m. at a place which I do not wish to name.   I suggested that it would be a good plan to fire on the police patrol car as a protest against the English occupying Ireland.   We arranged to meet at half past two p.m. the following Sunday 5th April, 1942 at a place which I do not wish to name. Initialled T.J.W.   I armed all the party and myself with revolvers one of which was a short Webley, 3 were Webley's and one was a parabellum.   We then proceeded to the Kashmir Road vicinity where police car patrols are very regular and we knew that we would see a car soon.   We were standing separately at two corners, two at one and three at the other. The car was then seen coming up Clonard Street towards Cupar Street and we ran into and Air Raid shelter on the Kashmir Road and when the car approached the junction of Kashmir Road and Clonard Gardens we all as I had previously instructed fired at the police car.   I had instructed all the other four men mentioned to fire three shots each but I only fired one.   There were about seven shots in all fired at the car.   I had previously arranged that we should run into Cawnpore Street entry on the right hand side from Kashmir Road and to hand our guns to three persons who would be waiting there to receive them.   (Two of them were girls.) after the shooting at the police car had taken place on the Kashmir Road.   We did run into this entry and saw the three persons as arranged and as we ran past we handed the revolvers to them. They were to take the guns away and dump them elsewhere but it seems that the girls for some reason ran down the entry as someone shouted that the patrol car was at the bottom and that a policeman was coming down the entry and someone else shouted that the policeman had seen him coming into the house which we ran into.   This was one of the men who was in our party.   I ran into the parlour and I heard the police knocking the next door the second one from Cupar Street.   I then grabbed my revolver from the brown leather bag which was on the floor in the kitchen. This was the bag we put the revolvers into in the entry and was brought to the house by the girls.   Someone of the eight persons (six men and two girls) said a policeman was coming into the house by the entry door.   I ran into the scullery.   There is a little glass enclosure in the yard and from the scullery window I could see a policeman coming into this enclosure with his gun drawn.   When he was about three yards from me and beside the kitchen window I pointed my revolver at his body and fired one shot. he staggered and fired back and I fired four or five more shots at his body.   The revolver I had was reloaded by me after it had been brought to the house by the girls.   No other person in the house had fired at Const. Murphy.   I then shouted that I had been shot.   I dropped my revolver and heard Const. Murphy groan and fall to the ground.   Constable Murphy's body was lying between the glass enclosure and the door which leads from the scullery to the kitchen.   I stepped over his body and ran into the hall of the house and there I fainted.   Next thing I remember when I woke up on a bed in the back room up the stairs.   Some of the party I had commanded said "What do you want us to do?".   I said "where are the police" and someone answered "they have the house surrounded" and I told them to surrender which they did.   About five policemen came into the room where I was lying and they arrested us.

Sgd.   Thomas Joseph Williams.

I have heard this statement read over to me and it is all true and correct and I do not wish anything to it or take anything from it.

Thomas Joseph Williams.

Belfast City Commissioner 20th June 1942.
Exhibited
Aldenagh Martin
Py. Clerk of the Crown & Peace.

Original typewritten statement made to the RUC by Tom Williams

Despite his initial reservations, Tom resumed command of the group and in the weeks that followed they settled down to jail life as best they could. They did not have to wait long for the trial to begin.

The trial began on the 28th July in number one court, Crumlin Road Courthouse. Seated in the dock were Tom and his five comrades. Weeks before, the charges of murder against their two women comrades had been dropped. The younger of the two, Margaret Nolan, pleaded guilty to a lesser charge and was released with a recorded sentence. Madge Burns was immediately rearrested and interned in Armagh prison. Interest in the trial was enormous and so the public gallery was packed with relatives and supporters of the six, as well as a considerable press corps.

The defendants were represented by Mr Cecil Lavery, reputed to be one of the best defence barristers in Ireland at the time. On the prosecutors' bench sat John Clarke McDermott, Attorney General for Northern Ireland. McDermott, then a rising star within the legal establishment in the northern state, was an ex-Unionist MP and Stormont minister. Having served as a British officer during the First World War, his unionist sympathies prompted him to join the B Specials in the 1920s.

The trial judge's unionist credentials were no less impeccable. Edward Sullivan Murphy was born in the Dublin area in 1880. Following partition, Murphy and his family moved to Belfast, rather than give their allegiance to the new Irish Free State. A committed unionist he was elected unionist

MP for Derry City in 1929 and went on to become Attorney General between 1932–39. A proud and devoted Orangeman, he held the position of Deputy Grand Master within the Order for a number of years. After his appointment he observed to a friend that no honour could have given him greater satisfaction. He was also a member of the No Surrender Club.

Much of the first day of the trial was taken up with jury selection. Both the defence and the prosecution rejected a considerable number of potential jurors, almost one hundred and fifty challenges in total, before the final panel of twelve was chosen. McDermott was the first to outline the state's case against the six. Taking almost two hours, he argued that, despite Tom's admission of sole responsibility for Murphy's death, all six were equally responsible for Murphy's killing. He had this to say:

> ...if a number of persons have a common intention
> to resist arrest by a police officer in violence, and
> in pursuance of that intention the officer is killed,
> then his killing is murder on the part of those who
> shared the common intention.[21]

Later in the trial, forensic evidence presented by the prosecution would show that only three IRA weapons were actually fired in the house. From these, rounds from only two weapons struck Murphy, fatally wounding him. Despite this evidence, the prosecution was determined that all six would swing.

Lavery then rose and presented the case for the defence. Unable to deny that at least some of the accused were responsible for Murphy's death, he instead argued that the six had acted in self defence and without premeditation. Their strategy, and only real hope, was that the jury would disagree on the verdict, murder or manslaughter, and thereby force a retrial.

The following day, the defence cross examined a number of RUC officers who had been present at the scene of the shooting, about the ill-treatment of the prisoners. Despite the overwhelming evidence that supported the allegations of brutality, Sergeant Lappin, Constables Allen, Smyth and Costello, denied that any of the prisoners had been assaulted. Head Constable Heffernan was the only RUC officer to admit, albeit reluctantly, that Joe Cahill's appearance after his arrest suggested that he had been beaten. Having first refuted the allegations, McDermott was now forced to justify the actions of the RUC:

> Even if seeing his comrade lying in a pool of blood, some constable did not treat Cahill with gentle care, didn't that point in another direction from that indicated by learned counsel for the defence? Was it not a two edged weapon? Didn't it indicate that the police regarded Cahill as being directly connected with what had happened downstairs in the house? [22]

Perversely, McDermott was now arguing that the fact that Joe Cahill had been beaten at the scene of the shooting confirmed his guilt.

The trial ended on the third day, 30th July, and the jury retired to consider its verdict. Tom and his five comrades were returned to the cells below the court. The prison guards provided bedding for the six, believing the jury would be deliberating all night. In the meantime the group settled down and were soon singing songs to pass the time and raise their spirits.

Much to everyone's suprise, after only a few hours, the jury informed the court that they were ready to return a verdict. That afternoon the court was reassembled. The court was silent as the foreman, Thomas Stevenson, rose to read the verdict. He declared, by a unanimous decision, that all six were guilty of murder but that in the case of Pat Simpson they were recommending mercy because of his youth. On receiving the verdict of the jury, all six young men stood to attention one by one and made a brief statement. Tom was the last to speak; in a loud and steady voice he declared:

> I am not guilty of murder. I am not afraid to die.
> There was no premeditation and I wish to thank
> my counsel.[23]

The black cap was then placed on Murphy's head and he passed sentence on the six:

> The jury have found each and everyone of you
> guilty of the wilful murder of Constable Patrick
> Murphy and I don't intend to say anything to you
> that would add to the horror of the position in which
> you find yourselves.
>
> The sentence and judgement of the court are,
> and it is hereby ordered, that you Henry Cordner
> and you William J . Perry, John Terence Oliver,
> Patrick Simpson and you Joseph Cahill, and you
> Thomas J . Williams, that you, and all of you, be
> taken from the bar of the court in which you now

stand to the prison from whence you now came, and that on Tuesday, the eighteenth of August, in the year of our Lord, one thousand, nine hundred and forty two, you be taken to the place of execution of the gaol in which you are confined , and then and there be hanged by the neck until you are dead and that your bodies be buried within the walls of the prison, within which the aforesaid judgement of death be executed upon you, and pray the Lord almighty have mercy on your souls.[24]

On hearing the sentence, the public gallery erupted with shouts and screams of protest and outrage. A number of people, relatives of the young men, fainted on hearing the guilty verdict. Almost immediately an appeal was lodged on behalf of the six and the date of execution was postponed pending its outcome.

Meanwhile, back in the jail conditions improved dramatically for Tom and his comrades. As sentenced prisoners facing execution they were now allowed to wear their own clothes instead of the prison issue uniform. Following their return to C wing they were moved from their single cells to the condemned cells close to the gallows. Instead of single cells they were doubled up in three separate cells. Tom now shared a cell with Joe Cahill.

On entering the cell, Joe found Tom stretched out on one of the two large hospital beds that lay along either side of the cell. With a large grin on his face he remarked to Joe, 'What do you think of this Joe, the great beds we're getting?' Unlike their previous cells, this one was clean and brightly painted.

SIX YOUNG BELFAST
SENTENCED TO
DEATH

CLOSING SCENES AT TRIAL

SENTENCE OF DEATH was passed on all six of the young Belfastmen who were last night found guilty of the murder of Constable Patrick Murphy, on Easter Sunday.

The execution date is August 18, 1942.

The condemned men are:—

Thomas J. Williams (19), house repairer, 46 Bombay Street;
Henry Cordner (19), fitter, 35 Malcomson Street;
William James Perry (21), labourer, 264 Cupar Street;
John Terence Oliver (21), painter, 167 Springfield Road;
Patrick Simpson (18), sheet-metal worker, 86 Cawnpore Street; an
Joseph Cahill (21), joiner, 60 Divis Street.

There was complete silence as the black cap was placed on Lord Justice Murphy's head, and then in solemn, measured tones his Lordship addressed the men. Addressing each of them by name, he said: "The jury have found each and everyone of you guilty of the wilful murder of Constable Patrick Murphy, and I don't intend to say anything to you that would add to the horror of the position in which you find yourselves.

"The sentence and judgment of the Court are, and it is hereby ordered, that you Henry Cordner and you William J. Perry, John Terence Oliver, Patrick Simpson, and you Joseph Cahill and you Thomas J. Williams, that you, and all of you, be taken from the bar of the Court in which you now stand to the prison whence you came, and that on Tuesday, the eighteenth of August, in the Year of Our Lord, one thousand, nine hundred and forty-two, you be taken to the place of execution of the gaol in which you are confined, and then and there hanged by the neck until you are dead and that your bodies be buried within the walls of the prison, within which the aforesaid judgment and death be executed upon you, and pray the Lord Almighty have mercy on your souls."

For a second dead silence lasted, and then the woman in the back of the Court shouted and the men drew themselves up to attention, made a right-turn, and, waving their hands and shouting a few cries, were led away.

Lord Justice Murphy then turned to the jury, told them that he would forward their recommendation to the proper authorities, and excused them from jury duty for a period of eight years.

The death sentence as reported in the *Irish News* 31st July, 1942

After the jury had entered the court and Lord Justice Murphy taken his seat, the foreman of the jury handed the Clerk of the Crown and Peace a sheet of paper.

Clerk of the Crown and Peace— Gentlemen, have you agreed to your verdict.

Foreman—We have.

Do you find Henry Cordner guilty or not guilty?

Foreman—Guilty.

Then followed a similar question and answer in the case of each of the accused.

None of them flinched as the verdict was announced. They appeared stunned, although a tremor passed the lips of some of them.

Each of the men, standing up straight and with shoulders back, were asked if they had anything to say.

Cordner: "That I am not guilty of murder. There was no premeditation. I wish to thank Mr. Lavery, Mr. Agnew and Mr. Marrinan."

Perry in his turn: "Not guilty of murder. No premeditation and no intention to kill. I wish to express my gratitude to counsel—Mr. Lavery, Mr. Agnew and Mr. Marrinan—for the fight they put up on my behalf."

Oliver: "Not guilty. There was no premeditation. I never intended to kill anybody at any time. I wish to thank counsel for the splendid fight they put up."

Simpson: "I am not guilty of murder. I had no premeditation. Kashmir Road was the only one to be performed. I wish to thank counsel for the splendid fight they have put up on my behalf."

Cahill: "I am not guilty of murder. There was no premeditation or intention to take life. I wish to thank counsel on their splendid fight. I also wish, through the medium of the Press, to thank everyone who made it possible to have such a splendid defence in this case."

Williams: "I am not guilty of murder. I am not afraid to die. There was no premeditation, and I wish to thank my counsel."

Irish News,
31 July, 1942
(see page 43)

The rest of the furniture consisted of two small tables, five plain wooden chairs and a large wooden locker that lay along one wall of the cell. Adjoining the cell was a toilet for their own use.

The PO (a Principal Officer or PO for short, was a senior prison guard) informed the six that they would now be under twenty-four hour watch: the death watch. There would be three prison guards in each cell with them, changing shift every eight hours. Joe Cahill recalled that most of the ordinary guards treated them in a kind and considerate manner, though there was the occasional 'bastard', who took great pleasure in their predicament.

They now ate all their meals in their cells. As condemned men they could order just about anything they wished. In addition to this they were allowed two bottles of beer or stout or two half measures of whiskey a day.

Each morning at 8am mass was said in a single cell close to theirs. Usually they were attended by one of a number of priests, Fathers Alexis, Oliver, McEnaney or McAllister. During their time on remand and indeed in the traumatic weeks before and after the execution, a close bond of respect and friendship would develop between the priests and the young men. While all of the group attended mass, Tom was undoubtedly the most devout of the six, a fact that left a lasting impression on the three priests.

Having washed and eaten their breakfasts in their cells they were allowed exercise in the adjacent yard. There were three periods of exercise each day, between 10am and 12noon, again in the afternoon between 2pm and 4pm, and again in the evening between 6pm and 8pm.

It was during this period that Tom wrote a letter to Hugh McAteer (see photographs), the new IRA Chief of Staff:

> Hugh, a Cara,
>
> Just a note to let you know how my comrades and I are getting along. I do not expect an answer as your answer to Joe serves us all in that respect.
>
> I am proud to know that you are our leader. My comrades and I are sure that you will use your utmost powers to free our dear, beloved country. And bring about the re-establishment of the Republic and its constitution.
>
> It is beyond the powers of my humble intellect, to describe the pride of my comrades, in knowing that they are going to follow, in the footsteps of those who have given their lives to Ireland and the Republic. To describe the courage and coolness shown when sentenced to death. As Joe has previously stated to you. Our sorrow is not being able to attack the court and the 'Northern' Junta. But now you know the reason.
>
> My God, can we tell you and our comrades who will carry on the fight, can we tell you of the gladness and joy that is in our hearts. To know that the Irish people are again united, aye, and well may England quake, Irelands awake, Irelands awake. After 20 years of slumber our nation will once again strike, Please God, at the despoilers who have infringed the nation's liberty, freedom and murdered her sons, her daughters, who have given us a foreign tongue; shall please God, strike and strike hard and make the tyrants go on their knees for mercy and forgiveness.

But shall we make the mistake of '21, no, no, tis men like you and your staff will see to it. That no farcical so-called Treaty shall in anyway be signed by a bunch of weak-kneed and willed Irishmen. Better that the waves of the mighty oceans sweep over Erin than take and divide our nation, murder her true sons again. Better would that the heavens would open and send fire to destroy Erin, than to accept another Treaty like it.

In writing this, dear Hugh, do not think that I am saying it to you or the gallant soldiers of Oglaigh na hEireann, it is from my heart that it comes to the weak- willed and ignorant Irishmen who may put any trust in England. My only regret is now I will not be with you in the fight and last stage of Ireland's battle for freedom. But with the help of God and His Blessed Mother we may be in heaven looking down upon our dear, beloved, tortured, crucified Erin, and look with pride on the men and women who will carry on the battle until victory.

Well dear Hugh I'll close with a message to Oglaigh na hEireann, 'To carry on, no matter what the odds are against you, to carry on no matter what torments are inflicted on you. The road to freedom is paved with suffering, hardships and torture, carry on my gallant and brave comrades until that certain day.'

Your comrade in Ireland's cause,

Lieut. Tom Williams,

'C' Coy. Belfast Brigade,

Oglaigh na hEireann. [25]

While morale remained high, these were difficult days. Lying under sentence of death, the pressure mounted as the day of execution drew near. But despite this pressure, the days were

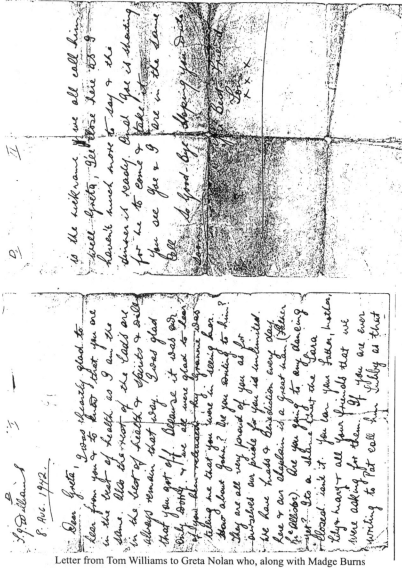

Letter from Tom Williams to Greta Nolan who, along with Madge Burns (Margaret McConville by her married name), assisted in the IRA operation immediately prior to the shooting incident at 53 Cawnpore Street. Tom writes, 'I was glad that you got off.'

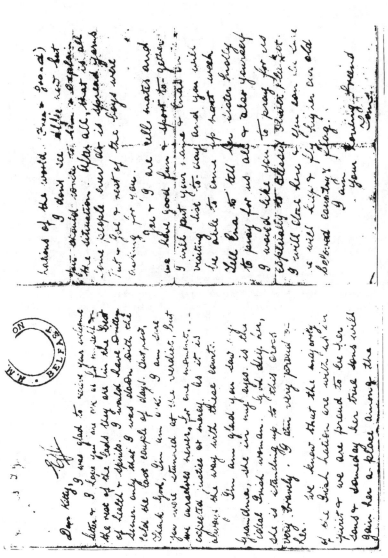

Letter to Kitty (above and overleaf), a friend of Tom Williams

368 N.I. Williams
Belfast Prison

Dear Kitty, I was very glad to receive your letter. I thought you had forgot about me & I felt little late than never. It is a pity that you did not ask earlier for a visit as I would like to have seen you. But if you could make it you could see us in court this week. Jack & most of the lads are keeping in the best of health & spirits. I saw Kathleen at first & would have liked to talk to her, but of course, that was impossible. At first I did not know who the P.C. was from. But when I got your letter I knew.

So Bread St it opened again at last. It is great. It was then that I first tried to lift a girl & attempt to dance.

But then I cant remember who she was. But I am sure she gave up & would dance after I had danced with her. (Put in its correct form if I had kissed the lass often.) I suppose you got a bit of a surprise when you Kind of Jack & I had been arrested. But it was about sleep. What Well find we have no regrets. What about Joe do you ever see him? I saw Joe to St Pauls now. Do you or Kathleen ever go up to St Pauls? Well Kitty I will keep hoping to hear from see you then.

All my comrades especially Joe & Pat were asking for you.

Your loving friend
Tom Williams

P.S. I hope you are in the best of health.

not without their moments of relief and humour. Joe Cahill recalls one occasion:

> There was one character in at that time, he was an old wino, a real Belfast character and he was up in C3. He would shout out when we would go out to the exercise yard in the evening. You'd hear him shouting out and the Rosary beads would be shook out, 'God bless ye boys. I'm say'n the Rosary for ye's three or four times a day. Would ye have an ole smoke on ye's?'

> And he would drop a line down. We would tie on a couple of cigarettes or a sandwich or something. He would pull it up and the Rosary beads would come out the window again and he'd shout, 'God bless ye's, ye's are great men. Long live the Republic!'

> One night there was a dead rat lying in the yard. He dropped the line down as usual and we decided we would parcel up the rat, tie it onto the line and send it up to him. So he shouted the usual greetings and prayers and he pulled up the line. Then there was a deadly silence and then an unmerciful squeal and he jumped up to the window and shouted, 'I hope they hang the whole fuck'n lot of ye's, ye's bastards.' [26]

When any of the six were being moved about the wing a prison guard would ring a hand held bell. This was to alert other prisoners to their approach, in which case they would remove themselves from sight of the condemned men. A constant source of amusement to Tom and his comrades, they

P.I.~~8145~~ 1548

3rd November, 1948.

Dear Father McAllister,

The magazine "The Sign" for October, 1945, which you sent to Convict Cahill cannot be given to him.   It contains an article on "Orange Terrorists" and I think you will agree with me that articles of this type should not be introduced into the Convict Wing.

As you know, we do not in the normal course of events raise any objection to the convicts receiving religious magazines, but if they contain articles which might foster or give rise to political strife they cannot be given to any prisoner.

I enclose the magazine.

Yours sincerely,

H. C. MONTGOMERY

Father P. McAllister,
St. Malachy's College,
BELFAST.

/MK

Prison censorship, 1940s-style

AUGUST 22, 1942   TRANSMISSIBLE AT NEWSPAPER POSTAGE RATE   ONE PENNY

DEATH SENTENCED BELFAST YOUTHS' APPEAL FAILS

Execution Date Refixed For September 2

IRISH NEWS

THE NORTHERN COURT OF CRIMINAL APPEAL YESTERDAY DISMISSED THE APPEALS OF THE SIX BELFAST YOUTHS UNDER SENTENCE OF DEATH FOR

Irish News
22nd August 1942

DEATH SENTENCE APPEAL FAILS

22 AUGUST 1942

(CONTINUED FROM PAGE 1.)

gether with the reprieve forms, are to be handed in this morning.

An analysis of the reprieve forms shows that the signatures include :— The Cardinal, two Catholic and one Protestant Bishop, 464 priests, 70 doctors, 50 solicitors and barristers, 10 Protestant clergymen, 13 members of Parliament and Senators.

In addition to these, many journalists, professors, businessmen and tradesmen from the city and the province, teachers, civil engineers, officers and other ranks who served in the British Army in the last war also signed.

REPRIEVE COMMITTEE MEETS.

A meeting of the Reprieve Committee held in St. Mary's Hall, Belfast, last night decided, in view of the dismissal of the appeal, to send telegrams to An Taoiseach (Mr. de Valera), Mr. Herbert Morrison, British Home Secretary; Mr. R. Attlee, Lord Privy Seal; Mr. Ernest Bevin, Minister of Labour; Sir Stafford Cripps, Leader of the House of Commons; and to Mr. William Gallaher, Communist M.P., requesting, on behalf of 200,000 signatories, their intervention on behalf of the six condemned men.

The telegrams state that the committee believes that any execution would only create and intensify bitterness at the present moment.

FORM 14.

IN THE COURT OF CRIMINAL APPEAL IN NORTHERN IRELAND.

———————

REX. *v.*   **JOSEPH CAHILL,**

(Appellant).

UPON CONSIDERATION being this day had by the Court of Criminal Appeal, as duly constituted for the hearing of Appeals under the Criminal Appeal (Northern Ireland) Act, 1930, of the Appeal of the above-named Appellant against   **conviction.**

The Court doth determine the same and doth dismiss the said Appeal.   **AND THE COURT DOTH APPOINT Wednesday, the 2nd day of September, 1942 for the execution of the sentence of Death upon the said JOSEPH CAHILL instead of the date appointed by the Judge at the trial.**

Dated this   **21st**   day of   **August,**   19 **42.**

J. M. DAVIES,
Registrar.

H6947/22 125 3/31 Gp3 O&S

Notification of the rejection of Joe Cahill's appeal
and confirmation of execution date.

referred to themselves as 'The Lepers'.

They had little to amuse themselves other than their own 'craic' and company. Reading material was restricted to religious publications such as 'St Alphonsus' Preparations for a Sanctimonious Death'. Even religious publications were liable to be censored as an official letter sent to Father McAllister in 1948 illustrates (see page 54).

They were allowed family visits each day following their trial and sentencing. While these visits helped pass the time and were unquestionably a source of comfort, they could also be a source of tension. Indeed such was the emotional strain that following one visit, Joe Cahill fainted as he left the visiting room. On one occasion Tom received a visit with his father during his period of remand. The visit ended abruptly when Tom angrily walked out of the visiting room, after telling his father not to return until he changed his attitude. A man of quite differing political views to his son, he had tried to lecture Tom about the IRA and its campaign. This was the only time that he would see his son while in prison and the last time he would see him alive.

Tom referred to 'a good argument' with his father in a letter to his uncle Charlie Fay:

> Dear Uncle Charlie,
>
> Just a note to let you know how I am getting on. I would write to Granma only I don't want to annoy her. I wish to thank you and Aunt Alice for the friendship you both have shown me during these trying times. I do not regret any action I have done

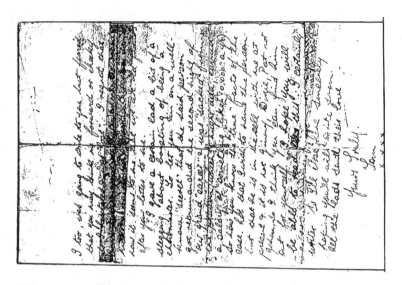

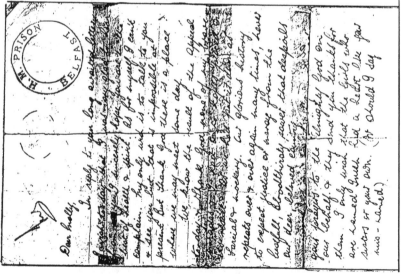

Tom Williams' letter to his friend Molly

outside, as I know and consider myself a Soldier of Ireland and anything I have done was my duty to my beloved country.

If it comes to the worst (as I'm sure it will) I will face my enemies with courage and spirit, which many gallant Irishmen have done this last seven hundred years. To die would be easy when one looks back at the men and women of our Nation who gave their lives gallantly and unselfishly.

As it stands at the moment we would be insane to think or even hope for mercy or justice in an English court. My comrades or I were not going to recognise the court but G.H.Q. sent in word to recognise it and we were left with no option. I know you may have got a surprise when you heard of my arrest and I'm sure you didn't know that I was in the Movement, but what Irishman (especially the young man) is going to watch his native Country enslaved without raising a hand to defend it from a vile slimy creature as England or watch his comrades thrown into jail, hung and tortured without raising a hand to smite down the hated lustful bloodthirsty hand of the British Empire. I am writing this letter to let you know that my heart was in the I.R.A. and to counteract any defamings (which England is noted for) that may come out or be circulated.

My trust is in my Heavenly Father and the Blessed Mother of God and all the Irish Saints.

I'll close now,

Your loving Nephew

Tom

Give all my cousins my love

Give my sincerest love to Granma, Father and Richard.

I have continued this letter next page.

I thought I couldn't write anymore but as I have this chance I might as well take it. We have been well treated since we came in here and it is not so lonely as one would think. As we are altogether in cells we are able to talk to each other until near dark by way of the steam pipe that passes through all cells. Then at early Mass or in the evening we are able to write to the Internees and talk to them. They send me over smokes every night, this paper that I am writing on was sent from an Internee called *******. I'm sure Paddy and Frank know him as he went to school with me. Also Charlie I would like you to thank ******* again for me for her kindness shown to me. She sends up a good dinner every day and two flasks of tea. I was glad to see you today and heartily glad seeing you got talking to Liam Smith. I haven't seen him yet and I'm sure he was glad to get talking to you.

If the raiding starts in the town again your house may probably get a touch so I would ask you to be very careful, because I remember an instance a long number of years ago when Paddy showed me an instrument belonging to you.

We are able to write to the P.S. [penal servitude] men, we slip them notes (God forgive us) at Chapel and most of the time it is at the Altar rails but as we shouldn't be in here I'm sure God does not mind because we cannot talk to them. The P.S. men are the long sentences. They were on strike last January and were badly treated during it. But as a reprisal for their treatment and suffering a warder was shot dead which in all accounts softened their stone hearts towards us.

I was very grieved when I heard what way my Father took it at first but when he changed his mind I was heartily glad, and I hope you have this letter before Richard comes down, you will be able to explain or show it to him and he will understand. I had a good argument with him the last time he was down about D.V. and the Free State Government which he upheld and I stamped on.

But everybody is allowed their opinions because if Ireland was in any danger from a foreigner they would join together in a common cause.

It is rotten when one is outside and hearing the Movement being run down when you couldn't open your mouth to defend it and if you did and were found out you would be C.I.D. for loose talk.

I'm having a smoke now, the way to get a light is by having flint and burnt rag which is called tinder and a piece of a razor blade. You spark your flint and the rag catches and you light your cig (providing you have one).

Within a few short weeks of the trial their appeal was heard by Judges Babington, Andrews and Brown. On 21st August the previous verdict of the court was upheld and the new date of execution set for 2 September (see illustrations on pages 55 and 56). Their only hope now lay with the Reprieve Campaign that was being mounted on their behalf outside the prison.

4

The Reprieve Campaign

Within days of the original verdict Reprieve Committees were established in Belfast and Dublin, spreading to other parts of the island in the weeks that followed. In Belfast, interested groups, such as the GAA, the Gaelic League, and other nationalist and labour groups formed a joint Reprieve Committee, and appointed Mr Eamonn Donnelly its secretary. With only a few short weeks to go to the date of execution, the race was on to save the lives of the six. The first act of the reprieve campaign was the gathering of a petition calling for clemency. Petition forms were sent to every parish priest in the North and placed at the gates of every Catholic church for signing following Sunday masses. Across the Irish Sea in cities like Liverpool, Manchester and Glasgow, petitions were gathered and sent to local MPs. When the petition was handed to the Minister of Home Affairs at Stormont on 21st August, it contained almost a quarter of a million signatures. It was signed by prominent personalities such as Cardinal McRory, three other Catholic bishops, hundreds of Catholic priests and a large number of Protestant clergy, as well as Sean McBride and a considerable number of MPs and TDs.

An intensive lobbying campaign was begun. Dozens of telegrams were sent to President Roosevelt and Prime Minister Churchill. Nationalist MPs in Stormont petitioned the British king. After a meeting in Dromnahane, North Cork, a telegram was sent to John Curtin, the Premier of Australia. It was signed by his first cousin, Denis Curtin.

With the IRA campaign virtually suspended, the call for clemency quickly gathered support. The Taoiseach, De Valera, met a number of delegations, including one led by the socialist and trade unionist Jim Larkin. Under pressure, De Valera instructed his government officials to intervene on behalf of the six young IRA volunteers. Supporters welcomed his intervention, despite being cynical about his motives. Earlier that year, George Plant, another IRA volunteer, was sentenced to death by a Free State military tribunal and executed on the morning of the 5th March.

U.S. Secretary of State Cordell Hull took up the case with the British government after being pressed by the Irish Ambassador in Washington. Hull spoke to Anthony Eden and Lord Halifax. The U.S State Department was urged by Senate and Congressional leaders to intervene in the case. Even the Vatican intervened, pressing the British government to reprieve the men.

By now the campaign for clemency was attracting support

from across a very broad spectrum. Mr. Louis. G. Redmond-Howard, the blind nephew of John Redmond, sent a plea for mercy to the British king and Home Secretary. Sir Hubert Gough, a retired British army general who had played a leading part in the Curragh mutiny of 1914, wrote to *The Times* on 14th August :

To The Editor of *The Times*

Sir – Six young men lie under sentence of death in Belfast. They have been found guilty of the murder of a policeman. There is no doubt that their trial and conviction were in due process of the law and that their acts, whoever it was that fired the fatal shot, had made all six of them guilty of murder in the eyes of the law. They are very young: their average age is 20 years. They have all protested that there was no premeditation and that they did not wish or intend to kill. Their actions sprang from quasi-political activities which I deem mischievous, misconceived, and injurious to Ireland. Of course the law must be vindicated. Of course order must be maintained. But must these six youngsters – all six of them – die because one man was killed? The law itself provides a machinery for the exercise of clemency to mitigate its excessive rigours. And statesmanship may well think that the cause of order will most wisely be served by a humane regard to the elements in the case which are profoundly stirring public feeling in Ireland. On all grounds I urge that mercy be used to temper justice.

Yours faithfully,

Hubert Gough.

71, Elm Park Gardens, S. W. 10, Aug. 14. [27]

The Reprieve Campaign: *Irish News*, 4th August 1942

DEATH SENTENCED BELFAST YOUTHS 5 AUGUST 1942

IRISH NEWS

NATIONALISTS PLEAD FOR THEIR REPRIEVE

NATIONALIST M.P.s and Senators, meeting in Belfast yesterday, addressed a memorial to the Governor of N. Ireland requesting him to exercise his prerogative and reprieve the six young Belfastmen condemned to death for the murder of Constable Patrick Murphy on Easter Sunday.

The meeting agreed also to request the Prime Minister, Mr. J. M. Andrews, to receive a deputation from them, which would urge a reprieve.

The petitions for the reprieve continue to circulate in Belfast. Thousands signed yesterday, among them His Lordship Most Rev. Dr. Mageean, Bishop of Down and Connor.

The memorial, copies of which were wired to Mr. Winston Churchill, Mr. Herbert Morrison (British Home Secretary), Mr. Eamon de Valera, Sir John Maffey (British representative in Eire), and Mr. Winant (the American Ambassador) was as follows :—

"We, the undersigned Nationalist members of Parliament and Senators of Northern Ireland, approach you with a view to exercise of your prerogative of reprieve in the case of each of six Belfast youths under sentence of death in Belfast Prison. With a deep sense of our responsibility we plead for mercy towards them. We submit to your judgment that the exercise of mercy would satisfy the ends of justice and also allay the anxiety and apprehension agitating many minds about their fate The condemned men are young, very young. Each avows that the death of the constable was wholly unpremeditated by him, and sorrows for his untimely demise with heartfelt sympathy and anguish

Trusting that your Grace will see fit to grant the prayer of this urgent memorial by mitigating the extreme rigour of the law."

SIGNATURES.

The memorial was signed by Mr. T. J. Campbell, K.C., Mr. J. Stewart, Ald. R. Byrne, Mr. A. F. Donnelly, Mr. P. Maxwell, Senator T. M'Laughlin, Senator J. M'Hugh, Senator Jos. Maguire, Senator T. Lynch, Senator T. S. M'Allister.

Mr. Denis Ireland, of the Ulster Union Club, was among those who yesterday came forward to support the reprieve petition.

The organisers of the petition are continuing to circulate it vigorously.

A monster public meeting, such as that in Corrigan Park during the anti-conscription campaign, is being talked of as part of the campaign.

CARDINAL INTERVIEWED.

His Eminence Cardinal MacRory, Archbishop of Armagh and Primate of All Ireland, was interviewed in regard to the matter yesterday by John Quinn and J. H. Collins, solicitor, Newry. His Eminence is at present on holiday in Greenore.

Ald. Corish, Mayor of Wexford, who had been attending the Irish National Foresters' Convention at Newry, returned to Dublin yesterday and interviewed representatives of the Irish Labour Party. He urged them to use their influence with the British Home Secretary to secure the reprieve.

Among the arrests made by police, in raids on Belfast houses on Monday night and early yesterday morning was that of a member of the Reprieve Committee of the Irish Unemployed Workers. He is still detained.

Another man was also arrested, but was released yesterday evening.

TELEGRAM TO T.U.C. CHAIRMAN.

The Unemployed Workers sent the following telegram to Sir Walter Citrine, Chairman, T.U.C., London—"Irish Unemployed Workers ask you to use your influence that the mass execution of the young Irishmen in Belfast jail will not take place.—M'Murray, hon. secretary."

Irish News, 4th August 1942

The Rev Dr. A. Wylie-Elue, Minister for May Street Presbyterian Church in Belfast, and five other prominent members of the laity sent a letter to the Stormont Cabinet calling for clemency. Considerable sections of the Labour and Trade Union movement on both sides of the border threw their weight behind the campaign. Paddy Agnew, Labour MP for Armagh, as well as the Communist Party of Ireland, asked the Soviet government to use its influence with the British government. Despite these many interventions the Stormont Cabinet seemed determined that the six would hang.

According to Tim Pat Coogan, Cardinal McRory approached Cardinal Hinsley, a close personal friend of Brendan Bracken, an Irishman and Churchill's wartime Minister for Information. Bracken in turn exercised what was probably a decisive influence upon the British Cabinet and Churchill himself.[28] On the days, the 26th, 27th and 29th August the Stormont Cabinet discussed the case. On Sunday 30th they issued a statement through the Governor of Northern Ireland:

> His Grace the Governor of Northern Ireland has considered the cases of Thomas Joseph Williams, William J. Perry, Henry Cordner, John Terence Oliver, Joseph Cahill and Patrick Simpson, previously lying under sentence of death in H. M. Prison Belfast and has decided; That in the case of Thomas Joseph Williams, the law must take its own course; That in the case of W. J. Perry, H. Cordner, J. T. Oliver, and J. Cahill, sentence of death shall be commuted to one of penal servitude for life; And that in the case of Patrick Simpson sentence of death should be commuted to penal servitude for 15 years.[29]

Whereas JOSEPH CAHILL has been convicted of Murder at the Commission of Oyer and Terminer and General Gaol Delivery holden at Belfast on the twenty-first day of July, One Thousand Nine Hundred and Forty-two, and the said JOSEPH CAHILL is now under Judgment of Death for the said offence:

And whereas it has seemed fit to His Grace the Governor of Northern Ireland and He is pleased to extend Mercy to the said JOSEPH CAHILL and that the said sentence of Death shall not be carried into execution against the said JOSEPH CAHILL and instead thereof that the said JOSEPH CAHILL be kept in Penal Servitude for the term of his natural life, and the said Governor has given directions for the carrying out of his merciful intentions accordingly:

Now therefore I, Sir Richard Dawson Bates, Minister of Home Affairs for Northern Ireland, do hereby signify the intention of the Governor of Northern Ireland to extend Mercy as aforesaid and do, by this Warrant signed by me, order and direct that the said JOSEPH CAHILL be kept in Penal Servitude for the term of his natural life.

Dated this 31st day of August, 1942.

MINISTER OF HOME AFFAIRS
FOR NORTHERN IRELAND.

To the Clerk of the Crown & Peace
of the County of the City of Belfast.

And to all Sheriffs, Gaolers and others
concerned in the execution of the
foregoing Warrant.

Notification to Joe Cahill commuting his death sentence one of Penal Servitude for his natural life. He was released after seven years.

Shortly before the statement was issued, Tom and his comrades were called to a legal visit. When they entered the room they were somberly greeted by their solicitor, D. P. Marrinan. He looked at each of them in turn and finally turned to Tom and said:

> I've good news for everybody except Tom. [30]

He then told them that all but Tom had been reprieved. There was a stunned silence for a few moments, and then Tom was the first to speak:

> Don't grieve for me, remember, from day one this
> is how I wanted it. I wanted to die and I'm happy
> that you five are going to live. [31]

At the end of the visit, the governor of the jail, Capt. Thomas Moore Stuart, and a number of prison guards entered the room and explained that Tom would be returned to the cell alone and that the other five were being moved to another wing, A wing. The five immediately refused to move from the visiting room unless they were given a guarantee that they would see Tom again before Wednesday, the day of the execution. A tense stand off ensued. After a hurried conversation, the governor informed the five that they would be allowed to see Tom before the execution – a commitment that was never honoured. With tears in their eyes, Joe Cahill, Jimmy Perry, 'Dixie' Cordner, Pat Simpson and John Oliver, each in turn, embraced their close friend and comrade Tom for the last time before they were led from the room.

Tom's five comrades were held in single cells in C wing

WILLIAMS TO DIE.; OTHERS REPRIEVED

Life Sentences For Four—Simpson Gets 15 Years

AGITATION TO CONTINUE

FIVE OF THE SIX CONDEMNED BELFAST YOUTHS HAVE BEEN REPRIEVED. ONLY THOMAS JOSEPH WILLIAMS IS TO DIE.

CORDNER, PERRY, OLIVER AND CAHILL RECEIVE LIFE SENTENCES. SIMPSON GETS 15 YEARS. HE IS THE YOUNGEST OF THE SIX, AND WAS RECOMMENDED

"ROUTED" SAYS ROME

REPORTED ALLIED LANDING NEAR CRETE

Sunday.

The Italian High Command announced to-day that a small Allied party attempted to land on Cerigotto (Antikythera), an island 25 miles north-west

Irish News
31 August 1942

overnight before being moved to A wing. Joe Cahill's cell faced his old one, the one he shared with Tom. That evening, through a crack in the cell door, Joe was able to catch a glimpse of Tom walking casually from his cell, with his head held high, whistling as he went. This was the last time that any of them would see Tom alive. The following morning they were taken to reception, where they given prison uniforms to wear and moved to A wing.

When the decision to reprieve all but Tom was received by the Dublin Reprieve Committee they issued the following statement:

> The reprieve of five of the six condemned men does not in any way alter the position. It is a half measure typical of Britain's policy towards Ireland.
>
> The Reprieve Committee will continue its work to secure the reprieve of Thomas Williams with undiminished energy.[32]

On Monday 31st August a massive reprieve meeting was held in the Mansion House in Dublin. The hall was packed to capacity and the crowd spilled out onto Dawson Street, stretching from St Stephen's Green to Molesworth Street. Mrs Tom Clarke presided at the meeting, which was addressed by Sean McBride, Chairperson of the Dublin Reprieve Committee. At the meeting he told the audience that there was still hope for Tom's reprieve and that nothing had so unified the Irish people in years. Mr Eamonn Donnelly, Secretary of the Belfast Reprieve Committee, appealed to southern Protestants to use their influence with the British and Stormont

DESMOND P. MARRINAN, B.A.   20, Callender Street,
    Solicitor.   Belfast.

                                      31st August, 1942.

His Grace the Most Noble the Duke of Abercorn,
Home Office,
BELFAST.

Your Grace,

Re: Thomas Joseph Williams.

    I would direct Your Grace's attention to the statement made by William
James Perry to Head Constable Hefferman concerning the murder of Constable
Patrick Murphy. In this statement he says "I then ran back up the Hall and
when I was at the foot of the Stairs and the kitchen door I heard three or four
shots from the direction of the Scullery door. At that time Oliver, Cahill,
Cordner, Williams and Patrick Joseph Simpson whom I had seen for the first time
that day were then in the kitchen. I then fired one shot from my revolver
towards the kitchen window. I then saw Williams staggering into the kitchen
from the scullery. He was moaning and I saw blood trickling down his leg and
from his arm. I then saw the figure of a policeman in Uniform in the back yard
moving towards the scullery door. Williams collapsed at my feet in the kitchen
and I dragged him alone into the hallway. At that time Oliver, Cahill, Cordner
and Simpson were in the kitchen and all had revolvers except Simpson. Then
three or four more shots were fired in the kitchen and Cahill then came to my
assistance and he and I carried Williams upstairs and left him on a bed in the
back bedroom".

    I strongly invite Your Grace to come to the conclusion that the fatal shot
or shots were not fired by Williams and it would be invidious to select him as
the one to suffer the extreme penalty.

    In these circumstances I would strongly urge Your Grace to grant him the
same clemency as has been extended to the others.

                            Yours truly,

                        (Sgd) DESMOND P. MARRINAN.

P.S.   Williams' statement was actuated out of a sense of loyalty to his
           comrades and his admissions are not borne out by the rest of the
           evidence.

A letter from Tom William's solicitor to the Duke of Abercorn:
a last ditch attempt to secure clemency (see page 76)

governments. Jim Larkin, William Norton TD, leader of the Irish Labour Party, a number of other TDs, and the Lord Mayor of Dublin, P. S. Doyle, also addressed the audience. The Committee recieved a telegram from Rabbi Zalmon Alony, of the Dublin Jewish community, apologising for being unable to attend the meeting but offering his support and prayers for Tom's reprieve. That evening a telegram was sent to Sir John Maffey, the British Ambassador in Dublin, asking him to use his influence with his government.

Meanwhile, all those involved in the reprieve campaign made a last desperate effort to save Tom's life. The day before the execution, D. P. Marrinan wrote to the Governor of Northern Ireland:

> You will pardon my further note. It has been reported to me that your attention should be directed to the fact that depositions proved that Thomas J. Williams before the police actually entered the room upstairs where the six were, had ordered his comrades to lay down their arms, the result, in all humane probability being that the lives of the police who shortly afterwards entered the room, were saved. I am requesting that this saving fact should be borne in mind to the youth's credit.[33]

That afternoon Marrinan sought an interview with the Northern Ireland Prime Minister, John Andrews, but instead was received by the secretary to the Stormont Cabinet, R. G. Gransden. Later that evening Marrinan was accompanied to Stormont by Mr C. E. Reddin, Secretary of the Free State's Licensed Grocers' and Vintners' Association, in an attempt to lobby for Tom's reprieve. That day, the Lord Mayor of Dublin travelled to Belfast to meet his counterpart, Alderman Black. On behalf of Belfast City Council Black told Doyle that, in light of the Governor's statement, there was nothing they could, or indeed were willing to do. A telegram was sent to Cardinal Hinsley urging him to intervene again on Tom's behalf. He acknowledged receipt of the telegram but replied that he had done all that he could. The Dublin Fire Brigade asked their Belfast colleagues to support Tom's reprieve. In a telegram they wrote:

> Comrades we were privileged to associate ourselves with you when death fell upon you from the skies, and we appeal to you to approach the Governor-General and your government supporting our submission, that while appreciating the clemency extended to five boys, that the gesture be completed by granting reprieve to Williams also.[34]

Father Burke, a former Chaplain to the Royal Irish Rifles, wired the Governor of Northern Ireland:

> Your clemency has staggered the world, don't destroy it by executing the boy Williams.[35]

The final meeting of the Belfast Reprieve Committee was held in St Mary's Hall in Bank Street. An eleventh hour appeal was sent to Churchill but there was no real hope now that Tom's life could be saved. The Committee called upon the people of Belfast to show restraint in the days ahead and to mourn in a peaceful and dignified manner.

To Father Alexis with sincerest love + prayer from Tommy. 2-9-42. Lieut C. Coy. 1st Batt Belfast Brigade Óglaigh na h-Éireann God Save Ireland

To Father Alexis C.P. who has shown me + my comrades great kindness + courage before my death. I will always remember + pray for you should I Please God reach the kingdom of Heaven. God bless you Father Tom Williams. Soldier of Óglaigh na h-Éireann 2-9-42. May God save + protect our beloved nation Ireland.

Tom Williams' note to Fr Alexis written on the day of execution

EXECUTION ONLY ONE DAY OFF

FEVERISH LAST-MINUTE EFFORTS TO SAVE WILLIAMS

Dublin Lord Mayor's Dash North—Attempt to See Governor

COUNTRY STIRRED: NATION-WIDE CAMPAIGN

BATTLES, "THE LIKE OF WHICH HAS NEVER BEEN KNOWN".

ROOSEVELT SPEECH

Washington, Monday.

President Roosevelt in a radio address to-day declared that the United States Navy is carrying out the command—hit our enemy and hit him again anywhere and whenever we find him.

Speaking on the occasion of the dedication of a new U.S. Navy medical centre at Maryland, he said: "To the removal from this earth of injustices and inequalities which create such tyrants and breed such wars this nation is wholly dedicated."

"WHERE IS THE U.S. NAVY?"

The President spoke of the "months without victories" follow-

series of visits with his close family and friends. All those who visited Tom that day recalled his great spirit and sense of humour. His young cousin Annie, who was only fourteen at the time, remembers him keeping the conversation going and trying to make them laugh. Before she left, he told her he would put a good word in for her with St Peter when he met him.

The last to visit him were his Uncle Charlie Fay, his brother Richard, his solicitor D. P. Marrinan, his former employer Gerry McGouran and his beloved Granny Fay. Thinking of their welfare, he asked them not to return to the jail the next morning but rather to attend 8 o'clock mass and pray for his soul. At the end of the visit he embraced each of them with tears in his eyes and asked his solicitor to convey one last message to his friends:

> Thank all for their efforts to save me. I am quite resigned if it is God's Holy will and if it is done for Ireland.[36]

Distraught, his Granny Fay was led from the jail in a state of collapse. That afternoon Tom received a telegram from his father. It read:

> Convey the following to Tommy – Be brave to the end, my son. Goodbye, God bless you.[37]

Tom spent most of that evening in prayer with Fathers McAllister, Oliver, McEnaney and Alexis. Before retiring for the night he wrote a series of short notes to some of his comrades and friends and thanked the priests for their kindness. On the morning of execution he wrote the note to Fr Alexis shown on page 76.

5

September 2nd:
The Execution

B y all accounts, that September morning was shaded by a dark sullen sky overhead. A silence lay across the jail. On such occasions the normal jail routine was suspended and so prisoners breakfasted in their cells where they would spend most of their day. Even the prison guards placed their heavy steel tipped boots upon the tiled floors with unusual care.

The confines of the jail were so quiet that the sounds from outside the walls would easily have carried across the slated roofs, perhaps even to the condemned cell. From the evening before, a large crowd had gathered near the jail and in the hours before the execution many of them knelt quietly in prayer. Throughout Ireland, Catholic churches were filled to capacity for morning mass. In many towns and cities, streets were blocked as hundreds and in some cases thousands stood in silence as a mark of respect. Nurses in the nearby Mater

Irish News headline, the day of
Tom Williams' execution, 2nd September 1942

hospital gathered quietly at windows to await the execution.

In the early hours of that morning the RUC had closed off the Crumlin Road to traffic, from Carlisle Circus to Agnes Street. Just yards away and behind the RUC lines, a group of loyalists had gathered, taunting and heckling the crowd. During the disturbances one woman was heard to shout, 'There are men being killed at the front everyday and they don't pray for them'. Others sang loyalist party tunes, 'The Sash', 'Dollys Brae', and 'There'll always be an England'.

Tom rose early that morning, dressed, washed and shaved. At around 6.30am he celebrated mass with Fathers Alexis and Oliver and again at 7.15am with Fathers McAllister and McEnaney. Fasting, Tom had refused breakfast and the offer of a last cigerette that morning, saying that he wanted 'the body and blood of our lord Jesus' to be the last thing he had taken before he died. Just minutes before 8am he was anointed by one of the priests.

Shortly before the stroke of eight, the cell door opened and the two executioners entered, accompanied by the prison governor and a number of prison and city officials. The main executioner, an Englishman, was Thomas Pierrepoint and he was assisted by his nephew Albert Pierrepoint. Albert Pierrepoint went on to become England's chief executioner, executing dozens of men and women during the course of his notorious career.

With two or three determined strides they were beside Tom. Usually seated with his back to the entrance of the cell, the condemned man was asked to stand by the chief executioner.

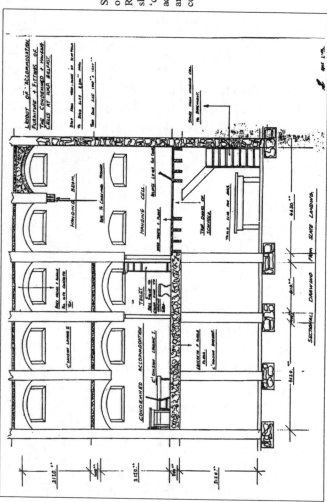

Side elevation of Crumlin Road prison showing the 'condemned accommodation' and 'hanging cell'

Thomas Pierrepoint then bound Tom's arms behind his back with a long leather buckled strap. It was said by colleagues of the Pierrepoints that Thomas Pierrepoint often sucked a boiled sweet as he calmly readied the prisoners for the drop. Both men were practised and efficient executioners.

As the buckle of the leather strap was fastened, the two prison guards present moved to either side of the large wooden locker which stood against one of the walls. The locker was lifted clear to reveal a door – the door to the gallows. It was standard practice to locate the gallows and condemned cell side by side. In order not to distress the condemned man or woman, the adjoining door was kept concealed until the last moment.

The chief executioner stepped towards the door and opened it, just a few short paces away lay the gallows drop. He led Tom through the door, while the other executioner walked behind him should he need assistance. He didn't. Without a falter in his step he calmly walked the last few paces of his life. As he did so, the rest of the group positioned themselves around the gallows.

Tom was halted when he reached a white 'T' painted in the centre of the wooden floor. For a few seconds he stood facing the noose dangling inches from his face. He remained calm. As the chief executioner pulled a white linen hood from his pocket, Father Alexis stepped forward and pressed a small crucifix to Tom's lips. As the hood was pulled down over his face he spoke aloud, 'Sacred heart of Jesus be my salvation'. The noose was placed tightly around his neck, while the assistant executioner strapped his legs together and stepped clear.

For a moment Tom stood there alone, before the trap doors collapsed and his small body dropped from sight. The trap doors slamming below would have sent a boom out across the jail, saving the onlookers from the sound of his neck breaking as the rope snapped taut.

After a few minutes the assistant executioner and a doctor descended through a small door into a room below where Tom's body now hung. The body was checked for signs of life and then left to hang alone in the room. On the Crumlin Road a notice of execution was pinned to the prison gates. It read:

> We the undersigned hereby declare that judgement of death was this day executed on Thomas Joseph Williams in His Majesty's Prison of Belfast in our presence. Dated this second day of September, 1942. Signed: Robert Henderson, Under-Sheriff of the City of Belfast; George Stewart, Justice of the Peace, for the City of Belfast; Thomas Moore Stuart (Capt.), Governor of the said prison; Patrick McAllister, Chaplain of the said prison. [38]

A half an hour after the execution, Tom's five comrades were led from their cells to the prison chapel. The jail was silent. So too was the chapel, except now for the sobs of this small group. One of the priests present began to say mass but broke down weeping and was unable to carry on. Another priest stood up and continued with the mass. When the mass was finished, all present gathered in the sacristy. It was Father Alexis who spoke:

> I met the bravest of the brave this morning. Tom Williams walked to that scaffold without a tremor

To Ever who receive's this
to pray for me always
& pray for the cause for
which I am dying

God Save Ireland.

Lieut T. J. Williams
"C" Coy. 1st Batt.
Belfast Brigade
Irish Republican Army.

Just before he was executed, Tom Williams inscribed the back of several
prayer cards such as the one above

WILLIAMS WALKED STEADILY TO HIS DOOM

"Could Not Have Been Braver," Says Priest

THOMAS WILLIAMS, THE 19-YEAR-OLD BELFAST YOUTH, WALKED STEADILY TO THE SCAFFOLD YESTERDAY MORNING IN CRUMLIN ROAD GAOL, AND DROPPED TO HIS DEATH WITH THE SACRED NAME OF JESUS ON HIS LIPS. HE MET HIS DEATH CALMLY AND WITHOUT A TREMOR, AND, IN THE WORDS OF THE PRIEST WHO ATTENDED HIM, "COULD NOT HAVE BEEN BRAVER."

BORDER INCIDENT

ARMED MEN OPEN FIRE ON POLICE

ARMED men, who crossed the Northern Ireland Border yesterday, opened fire on a police car which discovered them.

A police sergeant and a constable were rounding a bend near Cullioville, County Armagh, when they came upon the men, who had dismounted.

The police were greeted with fi...

JAP ATTACK ON SIBERIA

"MATTER OF TIME"

Washington, Wednesday.
The Pacific Council meeting at the White House to-day paid special attention to the possibility of a Jap attack on Siberia. Mr T. V. Soong, China's Foreign Minister, told the Council: "To us it is purely a matter of time before the attack comes."

"The Japs," he added, "are in readiness for such an attack." The Council also attempted to analyse Togo's resignation as Jap Foreign Minister.

Lord Halifax said afterwards that there was a discussion of the "particular possibilities of the Japanese strategists and what they have in ...

BELFAST MAN EXECUTED

SCENES IN STREETS

THOMAS J. WILLIAMS, the 19-year-old Belfast youth, was executed in Belfast Prison yesterday morning for the murder of Constable Murphy last Easter Monday.

At 7.30 a.m. Mass was celebrated in the prison, and, after receiving Holy Communion, Williams was pinioned by the executioner, and walked firmly to the scaffold. Death was instantaneous.

The authorities had taken elaborate precautions to prevent demonstrations in front of the prison. From Carlisle Circus to Agnes street, a distance of about half a mile, the Crumlin road was closed to all traffic, except tramcars, and police posted at the corners of side streets allowed only such persons to pass as showed identity cards and stated their business. As 8 o'clock approached crowds gathered outside the police cordon, and women knelt in prayer. Many of them wept. At the corner of the Old Lodge road and Florence place, women prayed on the pavement, while others on the opposite pavement sang "God Save the King." This was followed by cheers and the singing of "Land of Hope and Glory" and "There'll Always be an England." The police, however, pressed the singers back.

Police guards patrolled the district in which Williams and the 5 reprieved men lived. A crowd of women, singing Republican songs and waving flags, passed quickly up Clonard Gardens and into Bombay street, where every blind was drawn. The crowd paused for a moment in silence outside No. 46, where Williams had lived.

After the incidents at the prison the crowds moved down town to Wellington street and Donegall square, where scuffles took place, and later two men, alleged to have been among the demonstrators, were sent to prison for three months for assaulting the police.

At the Roman Catholic churches large congregations attended the 8 o'clock Masses.

LAST MOMENTS

Telegraphing last night an *Irish Times* reporter in Belfast said:—

"Williams was praying all the time as he walked to the scaffold, a matter of a few yards," stated Father Alexis, C.P., Ardoyne, who with Father P. McAlister, the prison chaplain, and Father McEneaney, St. Malachy's College, attended the condemned man. "He went firmly to his death without a tremor."

The interment took place in the prison burial ground at noon, with the three priests, the Governor, and a number of warders grouped around the grave-side, standing at attention as the coffin was lowered into the ground.

In a number of districts in Belfast shops were closed, and the Irish Transport and General Workers' Union men, particularly dockers, ceased work, while a large number of girls employed in the linen factories recited the Rosary in the Falls road district before they began work in the morning.

Late at night the streets of Belfast, particularly in the Falls road area, were being heavily patrolled by armed police.

IN DUBLIN

Irish Times
3 September 1942

Belfast Telegraph, Wednesday, September 2, 1942.

A DAY OF MANY INCIDENTS
FOLLOWS BELFAST EXECUTION

Gunmen Ambush Police Car Near Border

EXCITING street scenes marked the day in Belfast following the execution this morning of Thomas J. Williams, nineteen-year-old house repairer, for the murder of Constable Patrick Murphy on Easter Sunday.

A crowd which had figured in the recital of the Rosary and the singing of republican songs a short distance from the prison afterwards marched through the City Centre. They accosted two U.S. soldiers in Wellington Place and two men were arrested and later sent to prison following a scuffle with the police.

Then came a report from the Cullaville area of South Armagh, near the Border, of a police patrol car being ambushed and a sergeant being wounded.

The police returned the ambushers' fire but all the gunmen got away.

This afternoon a U.S. Army car was passing along Durham Street when it came under a shower of stones. The captain who was a passenger in the car was unhurt.

Outside the Prison

The police had taken special precautions to prevent scenes outside the prison. All pedestrian traffic was forbidden, only through tram, bus and other vehicular traffic being allowed through as from seven o'clock this morning.

Police guarded the entrances to each of the side streets leading on to the Crumlin Road, and everyone was turned back.

The authorities were determined that the disorderly scenes of the previous night, when crowds of young people gathered outside the prison and demonstrated, should not be repeated.

As each tramcar approached Carlisle Circus or Agnes Street police entered and gave the order that the first stop of this car would be Carlisle Circus or Agnes Street, as the case might be.

Thus it was that for an hour prior to the execution the outside of the prison presented a deserted appearance, and workers in heavily-laden trams and buses in endless procession peered curiously at the black jail gate, on which was displayed a notice signed by the Under-Sheriff and the Prison Governor that the execution would duly take place according to law at eight o'clock.

Meanwhile in the near distance could be heard the sound of singing and cheering. The strains of "God Save the King" were heard, and it was followed by tumultuous cheers.

STREET SCENES.

These came in the main from the Old Lodge Road end of Florence Place, the Crumlin Road end of which opens at most at the jail gate.

At the Old Lodge Road entrance an extraordinary scene presented itself. On one half of the road-way knelt a number of women engaged apparently in saying the Rosary and behind and around them, was a cheering and singing crowd, mostly of young girls. From the execution would, be

ately, tears coming into his eyes as he approached his brother.

He showed them the following telegram he had received from his father, who is in the Eire Army: "Be brave to the end, my son. Goodbye, and God bless you."

Williams asked Mr. Marrinan to convey the following message to his friends: "Thank all for their efforts to save me. I am quite resigned if it is God's holy will, and if it is done for Ireland."

Mrs. Fay left the prison in a state of collapse. She had to be assisted to a waiting taxi.

FORMER EXECUTIONS.

The last execution in Belfast was on April 7, 1933, when Harold Courtney was hanged for the murder of Miss Minnie Reid.

Altogether there have been seven executions during the past 20 years, including those of Williams and Courtney.

The others were:—

January 13, 1932—Eddie Cullen, for the murder of Achmet Musa (Turk).

April 8, 1930—Samuel Cushnan, for the murder of James M'Cann, postman, Toomebridge.

August 8, 1928—William Smylie, for the murder of the Misses Macauley, Armoy.

May 8, 1924—Michael Pratley, for the murder of Nelson Leech.

August 17, 1922 — Simon M'Geown, for the murder of Miss Margaret Fullerton.

THE MURPHY MURDER.

The murder of Constable Patrick Murphy, for which Williams paid the full penalty, took place at Cawnpore Street on Easter Sunday. A gang of youths fired at a police patrol car from behind an air raid shelter at Kashmir Road. Const. Murphy was in the van of the police who went in pursuit of the gunmen, and he was the first to enter 53 Cawnpore Street, where they had taken refuge. He entered by the back door and was found dead at the bottom, still clutching his revolver, from which the shots

Belfast Telegraph,
2 September 1942

Top: Prison record of Tom Williams' death by execution.
Bottom: A copy of Tom William's death certificate.

> in his body. The only people who were shaking
> were us and the hangman. [39]

For a few moments everyone broke down in tears again.
Eventually Father Alexis composed himself again:

> I've one other thing to say to you. Don't pray for
> Tom Williams, pray to him, for at this moment Tom
> is a saint in heaven. [40]

Shortly afterwards, the five left the chapel and were escorted
back to their cells. Exactly one hour after the execution, Tom's
slight body was pulled up and placed in an open wooden coffin.
A short inquest was held and as was customary in such
circumstances, all of Tom's clothes were removed , except for
his shirt, before the coffin was sealed. The cause of death was
recorded as 'Dislocation of the Vertebrae'.

Just before midday, Joe Cahill was called to his cell window
by a prisoner in the cell above him. In the distance Joe managed
to catch sight of a small procession carrying a plain wooden
coffin just before they passed from view.

The procession, now out of sight, stopped beside a freshly
dug, unmarked grave. According to a report in the *Belfast
Telegraph*, a number of prison guards who had accompanied
Tom's remains, stood stiffly to attention as the coffin was
lowered into the ground and quickly buried.

Greeves' Mill on Falls Road, now the site of a social security benefits' office. Tom Williams worked here for a period. The white-tiled Conway Mill, which is still standing, can be seen in the background.

The Irish News
AND BELFAST MORNING NEWS

No. 23,755   Estd 1860   BELFAST, MONDAY, APRIL 6, 1942   ONE PENNY

FIVE SHOT IN EASTER WEEK GUN BATTLES

Belfast Constable Killed : Others Wounded

I.R.A CLASH WITH POLICE IN BELFAST AND DUNGANNON

BURSTS OF GUNFIRE WHICH KILLED A POLICE CONSTABLE, WOUNDED TWO
B OTHERS AND TWO MEN FOLLOWED I.R.A. COMMEMORATIONS IN THE SIX
COUNTIES OF THE EASTER WEEK REBELLION OF 1916. CONST. PATRICK
MURPHY WAS SHOT DEAD AS HE RUSHED INTO A HOUSE IN CAWNPORE ST.,
A THICKLY-POPULATED AREA, AFTER SHOTS HAD BEEN FIRED AT A POLICE PATROL CAR.
ANOTHER MAN IN THE HOUSE, WAS WOUNDED, AND EIGHT ARRESTS WERE MADE,
INCLUDING TWO GIRLS.

While raiding a house in Dungannon, Constables
Forbes and M'Kay were shot by armed men, who
escaped, but bloodstains indicate that one man was
wounded by the police gunfire. Three men have
been detained in Dungannon.

I.R.A. commemoration meetings, at which armed
men acted as outposts, were held in several Belfast
areas, and it is reported that in the Cullingtree Road
area a quarter was made on a police tender approaching to quell this meeting, but this is denied by the police.

Police armed with rifles and revolvers are on
constant patrol in the Nationalist districts, and there
is considerable tension. The shootings in Dungannon
were condemned in St. Patrick's Church, Dungannon. Wreaths were placed on Republican graves
throughout the North.

BERLIN ON "THE COMING STORM"

Berlin, Sunday.

BIG FIGHTER CLASH OVER

JAP AIR ASSAULT ON CEYLON CAPITAL

Japs Begin Air Offensive On Ceylon

Allied Troops Make Another Withdrawal in Burma

Sunday.

R.A.F. fighters smashed the first Japanese air
assault on Colombo, capital of Ceylon. Tearing into
large enemy formations which attacked the city
this morning, British fighters shot down 20 aircraft
for certain, five more "probable," and damaged
another 25.

In Burma, where Japanese pressure is at the
moment strongest on the central front at Prome
it is reported that the enemy are about 100 miles to the
north, there has been no substantial change in the
situation during the past twenty-four hours.

All day yesterday the Imperial troops were
successfully withdrawing to their pre-arranged positions, north of Prome, were subjected to dive-
bombing and machine-gunning.

Enemy troops concentrating on the west bank of
the river together with artillery. Eighty miles
effectively shelled by Allied artillery.
to the east, the Toungoo front is apparently quiet.
Here, as on the Irrawaddy, the Allied forces are
in fierce of quiet and awaiting renewed onslaughts, still
enjoying numerical superiority, are expected to
launch.

[map showing PERSIA, AFGHANISTAN, CHINESE REPUBLIC, TIBET, INDIA, BOMBAY, DELHI, CALCUTTA, MADRAS, COLOMBO, CEYLON, BURMA, RANGOON, SIAM, THAILAND, SINGAPORE, INDIAN OCEAN]

FIRE BOMBS EXPLODE IN BELFAST'S SUNDAY SHOW CINEMA

"Whims Delay Ship Production"

Attempt To Burn Building Fails

SOME HOURS PREVIOUS TO A CONCERT BEING HELD IN
S THE HIPPODROME THEATRE, BELFAST, LAST NIGHT
FOR THE TROOPS, THERE WAS AN ATTEMPT TO FIRE THE
BUILDING WITH INCENDIARY TIME BOMBS, BELIEVED TO
HAVE BEEN PLANTED THERE DURING SATURDAY
NIGHT'S CINEMA PERFORMANCE.
SEVEN BOMBS ALTOGETHER WERE PLACED IN THE
THEATRE, THREE OF WHICH EXPLODED, AND IN THE STALLS
UNDER THE SEATS OF THE CIRCLE AND IN THE STALLS.
THE FIRST BOMB WENT OFF TEN MINUTES AFTER THE
LAST OF SATURDAY NIGHT'S CINEMA THEATRE-GOERS, AND THEN

REUTER and AP.

Crumlin Road prison, showing A, B, C, and D wings, the condemned cell and the place where Tom Williams was buried after execution

Condemned cell

Tom Williams buried here

D

C

B

A

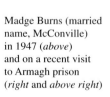

Madge Burns (married
name, McConville)
in 1947 (*above*)
and on a recent visit
to Armagh prison
(*right* and *above right*)

Above and middle: Joe Cahill's reception and discharge photographs
as found on his 'convict' file (see page 34).
Bottom: 'Dixie' Cordner's discharge photographs.

Discharge photographs of John Oliver (*top*),
Jimmy Perry (*middle*) and Pat Simpson (*bottom*)

ROYAL ULSTER CONSTABULARY
REWARD OF £3,000

The above Reward, or proportionate amounts thereof, will be paid to the person or persons furnishing information to the police leading to the arrest of any one or more of the persons whose photographs and descriptions are given hereunder, and who escaped from Belfast Prison on the morning of 15th January, 1943.

M'ATEER, Hugh, 76, William St., Londonderry. Description: Born 1917; Clerk; 5ft. 5in.; fresh complexion; brownish fair hair; blue eyes; oval face; scar on back of neck, scar on both knees. Sometimes wears small moustache but may be clean shaven.

STEELE, James, 70, North Queen Street, Belfast. Description: Born 1909; Plasterer; 5ft. 5in.; pale complexion; grey eyes; regular nose; thin face with sharp features; fair hair; sharp pointed chin; slight build.

MAGUIRE, Edward, 31, Whiterock Gdns., Belfast. Description: Born 1912; Slater; 5ft. 10in.; grey eyes; fair hair; fresh complexion; slight build; scar on thumb right hand, scar forefinger and thumb left hand, scar left eyebrow and top of head. Pock marked face.

DONNELLY, Patrick, Alexandra Gardens, Armagh. Description: Portadown, County Armagh. Description: 21 years; Labourer; 5ft. 7in.; blue eyes; black hair; sallow complexion; oval face; average or medium build; mole and scar on cheek.

Tom Williams' letter from prison (*overleaf*) to Hugh McAteer, IRA Chief of Staff, pictured above with four of his comrades

Dear S. Cara, just a note to let you know
how my comrades & I are getting along.
I do not expect an answer as this would
tie you down in all in that respect.
I am proud to know that you
are our leader. My comrades & I are bent
that you will see your utmost power to
free our dear beloved country. And bring
about the re-establishment of the Republic
& its Constitution.

It is beyond the powers of my
humble intellect, to describe the pride of
my comrades, in knowing that they and
going to follow, in the footsteps of those
who have given their lives to Ireland &
the Republic. To describe the courage &
coolness shown when sentenced to death.
We have been previously stated to you. But
sorrow is not being able to attack the
cast & the "hantich" Junta. But now you
know the reason.

My God, can we tell you & out
comrades who will carry on the fight,
Can we tell you of the gladness & joy
that is in our hearts to know when

II.

and well may England quake, Ireland
awake, Ireland's tyrants after 20 yrs
of slumber our nation once again
strike. Please God, at the deception
who have infringed the Latino liberty,
freedom & murdered her sons, let Ireland
who have given us a foreign tongue
Shall please God, strike & strike hard
& make the tyrants go on thinking
for mercy, & forgivness.

But shall we like the victims
of '21. No, No, No, Not like you & your
staff will do to it. That no foreign,
so-called Treaty shall in anyway be
dig'd by a bunch of wealth & widow
& women. Better that the waves of the
mighty oceans sweep over Erin, than
this and divide our nation, rather to
heaven would open & the fire to
destroy him, than to accept another
Treaty like it.

In writing this, dear Hugh, do
not think that I am saying it to you
& the gallant soldiers of the Irish no-

III.

It is from my heart that it comes to the weak-willed & ignorant Irishmen who may put any trust in England. My only regret is now I will not be with you in the fight & last stage of Ireland's battle for freedom. But with the help of God & this Blessed matter we may be in Heaven looking down upon our dear Ireland, trained, cherished this. And look with pride on the many women who will carry on the battle will victory.

Well Dear they. I'll close with the message to Óglaigh na h-Éireann, "to carry on, no matter what odds are against you, to carry on no matter what the enemy calls you, to carry on no matter what torments are inflicted on you. Up, mad to freedom so carry with spring, hardship & torture, carry on if gallant Grey comrades will that certain say."

Your comrade in Ireland's cause

Lieut. Sean William's
Belt... Coy Belfast Brigade
05?...? No-Surrender

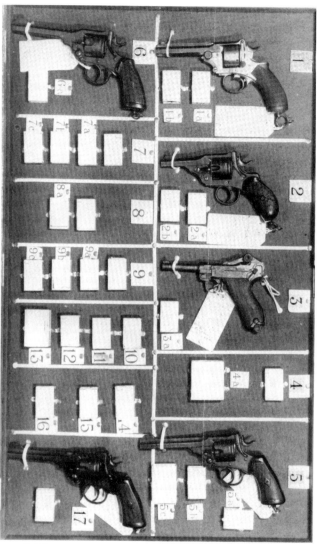

Exhibit of the guns involved in the shooting incident in which
Constable Murphy was killed, prepared for the trial of Tom Williams
and his comrades (see pages 28-29)

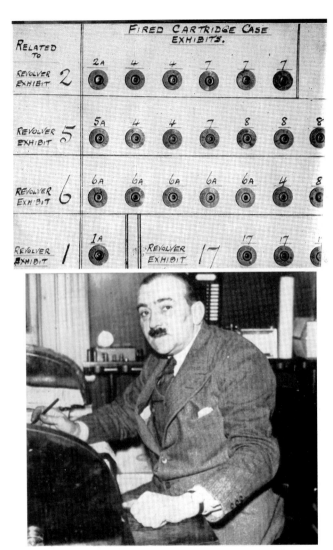

RELATED TO	FIRED CARTRIDGE CASE EXHIBITS.						
REVOLVER EXHIBIT 2	2A	4	4	7	7	7	
REVOLVER EXHIBIT 5	5A	4	4	7	8	8	8
REVOLVER EXHIBIT 6	6A	6A	6A	6A	6A	4	8
REVOLVER EXHIBIT 1	1A	REVOLVER EXHIBIT 17		17	17		

Forensic expert Robert Churchill who spent 2 hours 45 minutes in the witness box presenting evidence about the bullets and guns involved in the shooting of Constable Murphy. The trial date was brought forward to ensure Churchill's presence because he had threaten to resign his post over lack of access to scenes of crimes.

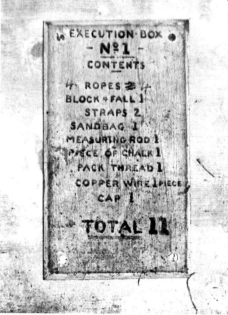

EXECUTION BOX
- №1 -
CONTENTS

ROPES 4
BLOCK + FALL 1
STRAPS 2
SANDBAG 1
MEASURING ROD 1
PIECE OF CHALK 1
PACK THREAD 1
COPPER WIRE 1 PIECE
CAP 1

TOTAL 11

These pictures, taken in Crumlin Road prison in the mid-1980s show two boxes of executioner's equipment (*above*). Inside the lid of Execution Box No. 1 (*left*).

Executioner's equipment including straps, sand bag and measuring rods (*top left*), hood (*above*) and noose (*left*). Note the seal on the noose which would only be used once and then buried with the person it had been used to hang.

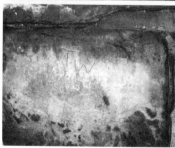

Top: (from left to right) Tony Curry, Gerry Campbell, Alf Doherty, Joe Cahill. Ann Murray, Harry Burns (R.I.P.), Liam Shannon, Brigid Hannon, Willie John McCurrie, Martin Meehan, Alfie Hannaway and Frank Glenholmes, pictured on the historic visit to Tom Williams' burial site in Crumlin Road prison. *Right:* Joe Cahill points to the stone with 'TW' scratched on it (above) which marks the spot of Tom William's burial.

"Judge me, O God, and distinguish my cause from the nation that is not holy."

O Sacred Heart of Jesus
HAVE MERCY ON THE SOUL OF

Lieut. Thomas J. Williams

ACTING O.C., "C" COMPANY
1ST BATT., BELFAST BRIGADE
IRISH REPUBLICAN ARMY

WHO WAS MARTYRED FOR
IRELAND, 2nd SEPT., 1942

AGED 19 YEARS

In *Crumlin Road Prison, Belfast*

R. I. P.

Far dearer the grave or the prison,
Illum'ed by one patriot name,
Than the trophies of all who have risen,
On liberty's ruins to fame.

"Oh! you whom I have loved so much on earth, pray for me and live in such a manner that we may be re-united in a blessed eternity.
St. Bonaventure"

O Sacred Heart of Jesus
HAVE MERCY ON THE SOUL OF

Staff Lt. Gerard O'Callaghan

ENGINEER, NORTHERN COMMAND
IRISH REPUBLICAN ARMY

Who died for Ireland 31st Aug., 1942

AGED 19 YEARS
R.I.P.

The dead who died for Ireland, the noble ones, the best,
Who gave their lives for Motherland, who poured upon her breast
In freedom's cause the blood she gave, who with their dying breath
Sent prayers to God to heal her woes, then sealed their love in death.

Above: An original Mass card for Tom Williams and Gerard O'Callaghan (19) from Cavendish Street, Belfast. O'Callaghan was shot dead by the RUC two days before Tom Williams' execution. He was at an arms dump between Hannahstown and Stoneyford and, according to newspaper reports was found behind a loaded machinegun which had jammed.

Right: Head stone in Milltown Cemetery

ERECTED BY
THOMAS WILLIAMS,
IN LOVING MEMORY OF HIS WIFE
MARY WILLIAMS.
WHO DIED 22nd APRIL 1926.
AND HIS TWO DAUGHTERS
MARY. DIED 27th MAY 1923 AGED 3YRs
SHEILA AGED 6 WEEKS.
ALSO HIS FATHER-IN-LAW
FRANCIS FAY.
WHO DIED 22nd OCT. 1923.
AND IN PROUD MEMORY OF
LIEUT. THOMAS J. WILLIAMS,
C. COY. I.R.A.
EXECUTED 2ND SEPT 1942
IN BELFAST PRISON
AGED 19 YEARS.

R. I. P.

Photo: Mal McCann

The grave reserved for Tom Williams in the
Republican Plot at Milltown Cemetery, Belfast.

6

'Carry on My Gallant and Brave Comrades'

The rest of the day was marked by protests in nationalist areas across the six counties. A large crowd gathered outside Tom's home, where a vigil was held. Black flags appeared across Belfast. A considerable number of dockers in Belfast, Newry and Derry walked out in protest against the execution. In Dublin and in other towns and cities throughout the South, businesses closed as a mark of respect, while the tricolour flew at half mast.

Following Tom's execution there was a flurry of IRA activity. From earlier that year preparations were being made to launch an offensive campaign in the six counties. Flying columns were being trained for surging attacks along the border. Weapons and materials were being moved into position across the North. During the course of the clemency campaign the IRA had in effect suspended their campaign in the North, to allow the appeal for clemency to gain the widest possible support. With Tom's execution they were now freed from any such constraints.

Just as Tom was executed in Belfast Prison, a column of IRA volunteers crossed the border near Culloville in South Armagh, heading for the RUC barracks in Crossmaglen. Seated in an open-backed lorry, the column were heavily armed with rifles, a Thompson sub-machine-gun, a Lewis gun and an explosive mine. The group planned to attack and capture Crossmaglen barracks. Significantly, they also hoped to capture a British army officer and hang him in retaliation for Tom's execution.

The plan was thwarted when the column encountered an RUC patrol outside Crossmaglen and a brief gun battle ensued. Believing that Crossmaglen barracks would have been alerted by the gunfire, the column retreated back across the border.

Other IRA actions followed:

September 3th – Bomb attack on Randalstown police barracks.

September 4th – Early morning gun attack on Belleek barracks.

September 5th – Gerry Adams (father of the current President of Sinn Féin), was wounded in a shoot-out with police in Sultan Street, Belfast.

September 6th – One RUC man and one Special shot and killed by the IRA near midnight in Clady.

September 9th – Detective Sergeant Dinny O'Brien shot dead at 10am at his home near Rathfarnham.

September 10th – John Graham and David Fleming, of the Republican Publicity Bureau, overcome after a gun battle

Belfast Telegraph, Friday, September 4, 1942.

Gunmen Attack a Police Barracks On Border after Cutting Phone Wires

Incident Follows Randalstown Bomb Explosion

ATTACKS on two Northern Ireland police barracks were incidents of what is obviously a new I.R.A. campaign reported to-day.

A band of armed men attacked the police barracks at Belleek, Co. Fermanagh, on the Ulster—Eire border, and after a sharp gun battle are believed to have escaped across the border.

Telephone wires in the vicinity were cut before the attack, obviously to prevent the barracks sending for any help.

So far as is known there were no casualties, but there has been intensive police activity on the border since the incident, the second frontier shooting episode this week.

The attack followed the explosion of a time bomb late last night at Randalstown police barracks, Co. Antrim, in which a sergeant was injured and a constable also hurt.

THE RANDALSTOWN EXPLOSION

The bomb explosion outside Randalstown police barracks at 11-15 on Thursday night blew in one window and surrounding brickwork, cut the heavy steel bars guarding the window as if with a knife, badly damaged adjacent houses and broke windows for a hundred

Inquiries at the hospital this afternoon elicited the satisfactory information that the sergeant was quite comfortable.

The dayroom is a small apartment 9ft. by 12ft., and how either the sergeant or constable escaped death is a mystery. The floor was

Belfast Telegraph, 4 September 1942

Many More Detentions as Police Swoop Goes On

A TOTAL of 89 persons suspected of being members of the I.R.A. have been detained by Belfast police since they began their widespread swoops in Nationalist areas of Belfast early yesterday morning.

The raids were continued last night, many of the young men being taken from their beds to police barracks in the neighbourhood and subsequently transferred to Chichester Street headquarters.

The only arms found by the police during the raids were two hand grenades.

Streams of parents made their way to Chichester Street this morning with food for their relatives. Some were carrying shoes.

Result of I.R.A. Manifesto

More than 100 people were taken by the police for questioning, but a number were subsequently released. Areas visited included the Falls Road, North Queen Street, Ardoyne, Markets, Docks, and streets in Ballymacarrett.

Armed with rifles, police cordoned off certain areas while their colleagues, revolvers in hand, went to houses and roused occupants, taking with them men whose names were on their lists and searching for explosives which may have been distributed recently.

It was stated that a father and five sons were among the members of one household taken for questioning.

This latest activity by the R.U.C. is a result of the I.R.A. manifesto circulated in Belfast on Sunday last, in which it was revealed that plans were afoot for armed attacks on British and American forces and the police, and the recovery by the police of the big arms haul near Hannahstown.

In a statement on Monday police headquarters said that quantities of arms had been sent out.

FIFTEEN MEN RELEASED.

Quite a number of the men detained during the raids of Thursday were interrogated by members of the C.I.D. at Chichester Street headquarters to-day, which was visited by high officers.

The "Telegraph" was subsequently informed that about 15 men had been released.

Later this afternoon 30 men were removed from the police cells and lodged in Crumlin Road Jail. They included 13 from country areas, chiefly the Lurgan and Armagh districts.

DETENTIONS IN PROVINCE.

In areas in many parts of the Province police had also been active, and this afternoon it was stated that between 40 and 50 persons had been detained for interrogation. A number of them had been released.

Two Men in Court

Patrick Tolan (34) labourer of [...] Act with the illegal possession of [...]

inside 463 Crumlin Road. It was a War News HQ; a duplicator and arms were found in a concealed room.

September 25th – Two small bombs exploded, one at the rear of Brown Square barracks and the second in Library Street off Royal Avenue.

September 30th – Ten minute gun battle on the Whiterock Road; one RUC man injured.[41]

Even before this offensive had begun, the IRA had suffered a series of set backs. On the 31st August, a friend and comrade of Tom's, Gerard O' Callaghan of Cavendish Street, Belfast, was shot and killed in an RUC ambush at an IRA arms dump outside Belfast (see page 96 and Mass card in photographs). In the days and weeks that followed, the RUC rounded up hundreds of nationalists across the six counties. Police searches uncovered a considerable amount of arms, four Lewis guns, nine Thompson sub-machine-guns, seven rifles, sixty handguns, a number of grenades and ammunition. The IRA suffered an even more serious blow when in the South the Gardai uncovered ninety two brand new Thompson sub-machine-guns, near Charlestown Co Mayo.

The IRA's problems were further compounded by the imposition of a night-time curfew in Belfast in early October and the arrest of its Chief of Staff, Hugh McAteer (see photographs). The IRA gallantly carried on as Tom had hoped throughout the last months of 1942, but executions on both sides of the border, arrests and continuous harassment were steadily taking their toll on a dwindling core of republican activists.

THE O'CALLAGHAN FUNERAL.

THOUSANDS ATTEND.

CROWD AND CAGE CAR.

Thousands of people attended the funeral of Gerard O'Callaghan, 170 Cavendish Street, the 19-year-old youth who was shot when the police raided the arms dump at Hannahstown.

The funeral took place from St. Paul's Church to Milltown Cemetery this afternoon.

Long before 2-30 the approaches to the chapel were thronged with people and as the coffin, covered with wreaths bound with green and yellow ribbons, was carried out women in the crowd recited the Rosary.

There was an incident which created great excitement as the procession moved up the road towards the cemetery.

A number of cage cars crowded with police were in attendance, and as one of these attempted to penetrate the crowd there were wild shouts, particularly by women.

Later it was reported that several young men had been taken into custody and placed in the police cars, but this was officially denied.

At the cemetery a large number of plain-clothes men took up vantage points on the fringes of the crowd, and the cage-cars were stationed opposite the gate.

The interment service took more than half-an-hour, and ended with the singing of a number of Catholic hymns.

The crowd then dispersed in orderly fashion.

The clergy at the funeral were Rev. Dr. Hendley, P.P.; Father Connon, C.C., and Father Toal, C.C., all of St. Paul's.

Belfast Telegraph
4 September

On the 15th January 1943, the IRA received an unexpected boost to its morale. Early that morning Hugh McAteer, Jimmy Steele, Pat Donnelly and Ned Maguire escaped from Crumlin Road Jail. As Harry White recounted the story:

> A plan was put together by Steele, McAteer and Donnelly. Maguire was brought in because he was a slater by trade. Noticing that one could pass from a trapdoor in a top-floor toilet, into the roof space, they worked for weeks on a scheme which entailed a bed sheet rope ladder, a wall hook swathed in bandages, and a tall demountable pole, the leather jointing ferrules of which were made in the boot shop. Even when they found the trapdoor padlocked, and an ordinary prisoner got to know about it, they persevered. On the morning appointed – "summertime" prevailed so it was still dark – they separately received permission to go to the wash house, where they broke a hole in the roof and escaped into the yard. From there they passed through to the wall fronting Crumlin Road, threw a sheet rope on which the bandaged steel hook was attached to the top, and on climbing that, they dropped to the ground at the gable of the screws cottages. In fact it was not quite that easy. The demountable pole for placing the hook upon the barbed wire on top of the wall, was found to be six feet short, and Maguire had to stand booted upon McAteer's thin shoulders. The other three had ascended and disappeared over the top, but when it came to Hugh's turn, he lost his grip and fell to the ground, severely injuring an ankle. However, he persevered, and with bleeding hands climbed over.[42]

Within a few weeks McAteer resumed command of the IRA. On Sunday 20th March the IRA received another much needed boost, when twenty-one republicans escaped from Derry jail. They had tunnelled their way to freedom. Despite these successes, the IRA was incapable of offering anything other than token resistance in the North. McAteer was recaptured again in Crocus Street in Belfast on 21st November that same year. By this time almost all the Derry escapees had been captured in the Free State, as De Valera ruthlessly stepped up his war against the IRA. Sometime before his arrest McAteer had told a friend:

> Any form of effective military action is now impossible. All we can do now is hold the pass until the jail gates open.[43]

7

Resonances

We now know where Tom Williams began and where he ended, and some of the events and influences that shaped his character in between. It has been much more difficult for me, from the confines of another prison cell, to find out who Tom Williams was, what he felt, what he thought, and what he hoped for. In this short book we catch only a glimpse of him.

With any such endeavour there is always the danger that the author may create a caricature. I have tried to avoid this. As all those who knew him attest, Tom was an exceptional young man. Considerate, generous, intelligent, dedicated, courageous – all of these things. But he was a young man all the same, still a boy in many respects, not a saint or super-human hero. Despite his courage, we can only but imagine how frightened and lonely this boy must have felt as the hood was pulled over his head and the noose drawn tight around his neck.

Tom's execution has become part of republican folklore in Belfast. The songs included in this book are still sung in the homes, clubs and bars of nationalist Belfast, over half a century after his death. Toby McMahon's play, himself another Clonard man, 'The 2nd of September', was performed in these H-Blocks by young republicans from all over the six counties. Occasionally still, 'Brave Tom Williams', can be heard in a canteen or cell during a session in H-Block 3 or 5. Tom's memory and spirit remains with us.

If the history of this small island were compared to a rich tapestry, then Tom Williams' story would only be the faintest of threads. Yet it is a remarkable story and deserves to be told. The story of Patrick Murphy, the RUC man whose life he took, is no less important, his death no less deserving of human sympathy. But this is Tom's story and Patrick Murphy can play no more than a minor, though important, part in it. Both of their stories are now part of our history, but the past is never completely dead; it continues to shape our present.

Tom's friend and comrade, Joe Cahill, returned to active service with the IRA, following his release from Crumlin Road Jail in 1949. He went on to play a leading role in the re-emergence of the modern IRA in the early 1970s. John Clarke McDermott, the chief prosecutor in the trial in 1942, went onto become the Lord Chief Justice, before retiring in 1972. In 1975 he was slightly injured in a bomb attack

intended to kill him. Six year old M
RUC gunpoint up the stairs of No
now Marie Moore to her married
Sinn Féin councillor in Belfast ar
of Belfast. Herself a lifelong repub...,
McConville, still lives in the Lower Falls area of Bel...
Two of her children, Mary and Gerry, went on to join the
modern IRA and served terms of imprisonment in Armagh
and Crumlin Road jails during the late 1970s, and 80s.
Jimmy Perry's daughter, Nuala, went on to join the IRA
and was arrested and convicted in the Diplock Courts along
with another young Clonard man, Danny McCann, later
killed by the SAS in Gibraltar. In June 1993, former RUC
Constable John Patrick Murphy, the grandson of Patrick
Murphy, killed in the shooting incident for which Tom was
hung in 1942, was shot dead by the INLA in Belfast.

In 1994 Crumlin Road prison was finally closed to
republican remand and sentenced prisoners. Only
occasionally after that did a republican prisoner pass through
the jail on his or her way to court, or on the final part of a pre-
release scheme. Over the years thousands of republicans
have passed through its gates. Only one young republican
remains incarcerated within its walls, Tom Williams.

Just days before Christmas 1998, in an emotional
ceremony, Joe Cahill was finally able to lay a wreath at
the spot where Tom was buried all those years ago. In the
years in between strenuous efforts have been made by many

ated individuals and groups, in particular the National ves Association, to have Tom's remains re-interred in he republican plot in Milltown Cemetery in Belfast. I share their fervent hope that Tom will at last be allowed to rest in peace beside his friends and comrades.

8

Postscript: Laying to Rest
by the *National Graves Association*

The National Graves Association has been campaigning since its formation in 1960 to have Tom Williams' remains removed from the Crumlin Road Prison and laid to rest alongside his comrades in Milltown Cemetry.

Some of Tom's old comrades have been members of the National Graves Association down the years; some have since died, but they never failed to keep up the campaign to have Tom re-interred and buried in Milltown Cemetery.

Through the years they have contacted members of Tom's family, first his brother. Then his brother died and the NGA contacted Tom's two nephews who live in the south of Ireland. Members of the NGA, along with Fr. Raymond Murray travelled down to their homes three or four times to see if they would do anything to have Tom taken out of Crumlin Road Prison, as this was Tom's last dying wish. They pleaded with the family, but to no avail.

As Tom, had been reared by his grandmother, Granny Fay on his mother's side of the family, the NGA went to a member of the Faye family, Anne Caldwell (Faye to her own name) and asked her to help them. Anne agreed to do anything she could to help, so we started from there.

The NGA then went to a solicitor, Joe Rice, of Victoria Street Belfast. He went through the whole case and employed a senior barrister, Arthur Harvey QC and a junior barrister to start proceedings in 1993 to have Tom's remains removed from the prison.

We lost the first court case as the Secretary of State for Northern Ireland ruled that anyone who was executed in a British prison would be buried within that prison precinct.

The lawyers took a judicial review on the grounds that the Secretary of State had the power to remit that part of Tom's sentence requiring burial in the prison precinct. The NGA had affidavits drawn up and signed by all their members along with Anne Caldwell and Tom's comrades who had been sentenced to death with Tom, but reprieved at the last minute. They also had letters from the late Desmond Marrinan QC who had represented Tom and his comrades back in 1942. Letters were then sent to all the TDs in the Dáil and MPs at Westminster asking for their help. Replies came back from some of these, saying they would be willing to help.

The judicial review took place in September 1994. Three judges heard the case and the courtroom was packed with barristers and the press who all wanted to see history made.

NORTHERN IRELAND OFFICE
Criminal Justice Policy Division
Massey House
Stoney Road
BELFAST
BT4 3SX

Tel. *01232   527523*
Fax. *01232   527507*

Messrs John J Rice & Co
Law Society House
94 Victoria Street
BELFAST
BT1 3JZ.

Your Ref: NB/JC/MSC882
30 August 1995

Dear Sirs

The case of the late Thomas Williams

Thank you for your letters of 7 and 22 August 1995 about the exhumation of the remains of Thomas Williams.

I am pleased to tell you that Her Majesty has signed the Warrant for Remission, which will now be forwarded to the Governor of Belfast Prison.

Yours sincerely

A. McKechnie

AMcKechnie

Letter from the Northern Ireland Office, following the court case removing the legal obstacle preventing Tom Williams' remains being removed from Crumlin Road prison

The lawyers fought an historic case and quoted the *Bentley* case in England. Finally, the case was won and the judges ruled that Tom's remains could be taken and re-buried in consecrated ground in Milltown Cemetery. The old British laws of 1868, which required the burial of anyone executed within the prison walls were swept aside.

The case received a lot of press coverage. The NGA then applied to the Northern Ireland Office to take Tom's remains out of the prison. The authorities replied that Tom's remains would have to be removed by his immediate family or by the NGA acting with the authority of the family. The two nephews then refused to have the NGA involved, so things were once more at a standstill.

After some time, it came to our attention that Tom had a half sister in England and two half brothers, one in Denmark and the other in Canada. So they were contacted and seemed interested in helping, even though they never knew Tom. The half sister, Anne, came over and talked to other members of the Williams' family and agreed to have Tom buried in his mother's grave in Milltown Cemetery. The NGA was delighted that at least Tom would be brought to Milltown, even though we would have preferred that he was buried alongside his comrades in the republican plot.

Since then, numerous letters have been written to Tom's half sister Anne and half brother Philip, saying the NGA would like to take part in Tom's funeral, but these letters have never been answered. We did hear that the Williams' family were going to have a private funeral, but four years have passed and still no sign of the family moving.

In December 1998, the NGA wrote to the Northern Ireland Office requesting permission to lay a wreath at Tom's grave inside the prison, as no-one had been allowed to pay their respects in the last 57 years. A letter came back from the NIO agreeing to let the NGA into Crumlin Road Prison to lay a wreath (see photographs).

On 11 December 1998, the National Graves Association had a commemoration and laid wreaths at site of Tom's burial in Crumlin Road Prison. This was an historical and emotional moment for all who attended, and particularly for Tom's comrade, Joe Cahill.

Postscript

I n early 1991 I chaired a meeting of representatives of the broad republican family from the greater Belfast area. Among those present were two representatives of the National Graves Association. They informed the meeting that the NGA intended to prioritise and intensify the campaign for the release of the remains of Tom Williams from Crumlin Road Jail. The following year, 1992, would mark the 50th anniversary of Tom's execution. By the end of 1991 I would be back in Crumlin Road Jail myself, having been imprisoned along with two comrades, Jim McVeigh and Tony O'Neill. The wings and cells of 'The Crum' are silent keepers of important volumes of the history of republican resistance over decades.

This sense of history and its significance were never lost on me. I had been familiar with The Crum long before I ever really knew where exactly it was or what it really looked like. I first saw and visited The Crum in 1970 when my eldest brother was held there for a short period. I would revisit it many times in later years and be held on each of its four wings as a republican prisoner on several occasions.

I have been an active republican from my early teenage years. My father has been an active republican in one way or another all his adult life. Figures who were to become republican legends in Belfast and beyond were part of my childhood. Men and women such as Seamus Twomey, Albert Price and Máire Drumm, were all familiar people and names to me. Equally familiar names were those of Tom Williams, Gerard O'Callaghan and Seamus 'Rocky'' Burns.

In ways I have been fortunate that the spirit of resistance that has been the hallmark of the republican struggle has always been around me. Gerard O'Callaghan was a neighbour of my mother and her family when they lived in Cavendish Street. He was ambushed and killed on the property of Jack McCaffery's family at Hannastown. Jack and his family lived in a house behind my parents home. Rocky Burns was a friend and comrade of my father. Tom Williams was a comrade to each of them.

During our time on remand in The Crum in 1992 we commemorated the 50th anniversary of Tom Williams' execution. We marked the event with a small ceremony in the canteen on the top landing of A Wing. One of the lads concluded the ceremony with the singing of the ballad of Tom Williams. From our cell windows we could see out over the exercise yard wall towards the prison hospital and across to the area of the old wood yard wall towards the prison hospital and across to the area of the old wood yard, where the burial place was situated.

I had been in C Wing for a period back in 1977 where the condemned cell and scaffold were located on C1, the bottom landing. Fifty years after Tom Williams left that cell and stood upon the scaffold I was perched at another cell window in A Wing looking across to where his body lay. I can remember reflecting on the fact that Tony, who was imprisoned along with Jim and I, was only eighteen years old – the same age Tom was when he was imprisoned.

Anyone who has been on the inside of The Crum or a similar prison will have experienced the coldness, the silence and the feeling of total isolation that can permeate these victorian institutions. When Tom Williams walked that short distance to the place of his death these feelings must have been almost overpowering. I think that most, if not all, republican prisoners will have often sought strength and solace from the sacrifice of comrades like Tom Wiliams. Those beliefs and their sacrifice continue to sustain us.

In December 1994 Volunteer Pol Kinsella died while a prisoner in the H-Blocks of Long Kesh. He was with us in The Crum in 1992. It is my sincerest hope that Pol will be the last republican to die on the inside of prison walls.

The men and women of the National Graves Association, the friends and comrades of Tom Williams, never gave up hope. They were determined to bring his remains home. They never faltered. They perservered against massive odds.

The Crum has now closed. The court where Tom and his comrades, and many more of us, were put on trial and sentenced, is now closed. The underground tunnel from The Crum to the court will carry no more prisoners. Tom Williams was the last republican prisoner to be hanged in the six counties.

The release of all political prisoners as part of the peace process is under way. No women comrades remain in prison. All republican prisoners held in prisons in England have been repatriated. Only the H-Blocks and Portlaoise hold republican prisoners at present. Tom Williams is the last republican prisoner to be held in Crumlin Road Jail. His final release would mark the completion of a significant and proud chapter in the history of the republican struggle.

Padraic Wilson
OC Republican POWs
H-Blocks, Long Kesh, April 1999

Appendix
The British Government's
Instructions for Executions

(BY ORDER OF THE SECRETARY OF STATE, THIS
DOCUMENT IS TO BE TREATED AS MOST STRICTLY
CONFIDENTIAL, BUT THE RESPONSIBLE WORKS
OFFICER SHOULD BE GIVEN THE OPPORTUNITY TO
STUDY ITS CONTENTS. IN ANY CASE WHEN A COPY
IS SUPPLIED TO A SHERIFF HE IS REQUESTED TO
RETURN IT TO THE PRISON GOVERNOR FROM WHOM
HE RECEIVED IT.)

MEMORANDUM OF INSTRUCTIONS
FOR CARRYING OUT AN EXECUTION

1. The trap doors shall be stained a dark colour and their outer
edges shall be defined by a white line three inches broad painted
round the edge of the pit outside the traps.

2. (a) A week before an execution the apparatus for the
execution shall be tested in the following manner under the
supervision of the Works Officer, the governor being present:-

The working of the scaffold will first be tested without a weight. Then a bag of dry sand of the same weight as the culprit will be attached to the rope and so adjusted as to allow the bag a drop equal to, or rather more than, that which the culprit should receive, so that the rope may be stretched with a force of not more than 1,000 foot-pounds. See table of drops. The working of the apparatus under these conditions will then be tested. The bag must be of the approved pattern, with a thick and well padded neck, so as to prevent an injury to the rope and leather. Towelling will be supplied for padding the neck of the bag under the noose. As the gutta percha round the noose end of the execution ropes hardens in cold weather, care should be taken to have it warmed and manipulated immediately before the bag is tested.

(b) On the day before the execution the apparatus shall be tested again as above, the Works Officer and the executioner being present. For the purpose of this test a note of the weight and height of the culprit should be obtained from the Medical Officer and handed to the executioner.

3. After the completion of each test the scaffold and all the appliances will be locked up, the key kept by the Governor or other responsible officer; but the bag of sand should remain suspended all the night preceding the execution so as to take the stretch out of the rope.

4. The executioner and any persons appointed to assist in the operation should make themselves thoroughly acquainted with the workings of the apparatus.

5. In order to prevent accidents during the preliminary tests and procedure the lever will be fixed by a safety-pin, and the Works or other Prison Officer charged with the care of the

EXECUTIONS.—Table of Drops (October, 1913)

The length of the drop may usually be calculated by dividing 1,000 foot-pounds by the weight of the culprit and his clothing in pounds, which will give the length of the drop in feet, but no drop should exceed 8 feet 6 inches. Thus a person weighing 150 pounds in his clothing will ordinarily require a drop of 1,000 divided by 150=6⅔ feet, *i.e.*, 6 feet 8 inches. The following table is calculated on this basis up to the weight of 200 pounds:—

TABLE OF DROPS

Weight of the Prisoner in his Clothes	Length of the Drop		Weight of the Prisoner in his Clothes	Length of the Drop		Weight of the Prisoner in his Clothes	Length of the Drop	
lbs.	ft.	ins.	lbs.	ft.	ins.	lbs.	ft.	ins.
118 and under	8	6	138 and under	7	3	167 and under	6	0
119 ,,	8	5	140 ,,	7	2	169 ,,	5	11
120 ,,	8	4	141 ,,	7	1	171 ,,	5	10
121 ,,	8	3	143 ,,	7	0	174 ,,	5	9
122 ,,	8	2	145 ,,	6	11	176 ,,	5	8
124 ,,	8	1	146 ,,	6	10	179 ,,	5	7
125 ,,	8	0	148 ,,	6	9	182 ,,	5	6
126 ,,	7	11	150 ,,	6	8	185 ,,	5	5
128 ,,	7	10	152 ,,	6	7	188 ,,	5	4
129 ,,	7	9	154 ,,	6	6	190 ,,	5	3
130 ,,	7	8	156 ,,	6	5	194 ,,	5	2
132 ,,	7	7	158 ,,	6	4	197 ,,	5	1
133 ,,	7	6	160 ,,	6	3	200 ,,	5	0
135 ,,	7	5	162 ,,	6	2			
136 ,,	7	4	164 ,,	6	1			

apparatus prior to the execution will be responsible for seeing that the pin is properly in position both before and after the tests. The responsibility for withdrawing the pin at the execution will rest on the executioner.

6.   Death by hanging ought to result from dislocation of the neck. The length of the drop will be determined in accordance with the attached Table of Drops.

7.   The required length of rope is regulated as follows:-

(a)   At the end of the rope which forms the noose the executioner should see that 13 inches from the centre of the ring are marked off by twine wrapped round the covering; this is the fixed quantity, which, with the stretching of this position of the rope, and the lengthening of the neck and body of the culprit, will represent the average depth of the head and circumference of the neck after constriction.

(b)   While the bag of sand is still suspended, the executioner will measure off from twine wrapped round on the rope the required length of the drop and will make a chalk mark on the rope at the end of this length. A piece of copper wire fastened to the chain will now be stretched down the rope till it reaches the chalk mark, and will be cut off there so that the cut end of the copper wire shall terminate at the upper end of the measured length of the drop. The bag of sand will then be raised from the pit, and disconnected from the rope.

The chain will now be so adjusted at the bracket that the lower end of the copper wire shall reach to the same level from the floor of the scaffold as the height of the prisoner. The known height of the prisoner can be readily measured on the scaffold by a graduated rule of six foot ix inches long. When the chain has been raised to the proper height the cotter must be securely fixed through the bracket and chain. The executioner will now make a chalk mark on the floor of the scaffold, in a plumb line with the chain, where the prisoner should stand.

(c) These details will be attended to as soon as possible after 6a.m. on the day of the execution so as to allow the rope time to regain a portion of its elasticity before the execution, and, if possible, the gutta percha on the rope should again be warmed.

8. The copper wire will now be detached, and after allowing sufficient amount of rope should be fastened to the chain above the level of the head of the culprit with a pack-thread. The pack-thread should be strong enough to support the rope without breaking.

9. When all the preparations are completed the scaffold will remain in the charge of a responsible officer until the time is fixed for the execution.

10. At the time fixed for the execution, the executioner will go to the pinioning room, which should be as close as practicable to the scaffold, and there apply the apparatus. When the culprit is pinioned and his neck is bared he will be at once conducted to the scaffold.

11. On reaching the scaffold the procedure will be as follows:-

(a)   The executioner will:-

(i)   Place the culprit exactly under the part of the beam to which the rope is attached.
(ii) Put the white linen cap on the culprit.
(iii) Put on the rope round the neck quite tightly (with the

cap between the rope and the neck), the metal eye being directed forwards, and placed in front of the angle of the lower jaw, so that with the constriction of the neck it may come underneath the chin. The noose should be kept tight by means of a stiff leather washer, or an india rubber washer, or a wedge.

(b) While the executioner is carrying out the procedure in paragraph (a) the assistant executioner will:-

(i)   Strap the culprits legs tightly.
(ii)   Step back beyond the white safety line so as to be well clear of the trap doors.
(iii) Give an agreed visual signal to the executioner to show that he is clear.

(c) On receipt of the signal from his assistant, the executioner will:-

(i)   Withdraw the safety pin.
(ii)   Pull the lever which lets down the trap doors.

12. The body will hang for a minimum of 45 minutes, and will then be carefully raised from the pit provided the Medical Officer declares life to be extinct. Then the body will be detached from the rope and removed to the place set aside for the Coroner's inspection, a careful record having first been made and given to the medical examiner of both the initial and final drops. The rope will be removed from the neck, and also the straps from the body. In laying out the body for the inquest the head will be raised three inches by placing a small piece of wood under it.

MEMORANDUM OF CONDITIONS TO WHICH ANY PERSON ACTING AS ASSISTANT EXECUTIONER IS REQUIRED TO CONFORM.

(An Assistant Executioner will not be employed by the Governor without the concurrence of the High Sheriff.)

1. An Assistant Executioner is engaged, with the concurrence of the High Sheriff, by the Governor of the prison in which the execution is to take place, and is required to conform with any instructions he may receive from or on behalf of the High Sheriff in connection with any execution for which he may be engaged.

2. A list of persons competent for the office of Assistant Executioner is to be in the possession of High Sheriffs and Governors: it is therefore unnecessary for any person to make application for employment in connection with an execution, and such application will be regarded as objectionable conduct and may lead to the removal of the applicant's name from the list.

3. Any person engaged as an Assistant Executioner will report himself at the prison at which an execution for which he has been engaged is to take place not later than 4 o'clock on the afternoon preceding the day of the execution.

4. He is required to remain in the prison from the time of his arrival until the completion of the execution and until permission is given for him to leave.

5. During the time he remains in the prison he will be provided with lodgings and maintenance on an approval scale.

6. He should avoid attracting public attention in going to or from the prison; he should clearly understand that his conduct and general behaviour must be respectable and discreet, not only at the place and time of execution, but before and subsequently; in particular he must not give to any person particulars on the subject of his duty for publication.

7. His remuneration will be £1 - 11s - 6d, for the performance of the duty required of him, to which will be added £1 - 11s - 6d, if his conduct and behaviour is satisfactory. The latter part of the fee will not be made payable until a fortnight after the execution has taken place.

8. Record will be kept of his conduct and efficiency on each occasion of his being employed, and this record will be at the disposal of any Governor who may have to engage an assistant executioner.

9. The name of any person who does not give satisfaction, or whose conduct is in any way objectionable, so as to cast discredit on himself, either in connection with the duties or otherwise, will be removed from the list.

10. The apparatus approval for use at executions will be provided at the prison, and no apparatus other than the approved apparatus must be used in connection with any execution.

11. The Assistant Executioner will give such information, or make such record of the occurrences as the Governor of the prison may require.

Footnotes and Sources

1. Michael Farrell, *The Orange State*, p. 81.
2. *Ibid*, p. 95.
3. Jonathan Bardon, *A History of Ulster*, p. 494.
4. *Ibid*, p. 493.
5. Taken from a letter from Leo Wilson.
6. According to Cormac O' Grada in *The Rocky Road*, in the early 1900s TB killed more than 11,500 people every year in Ireland. Slum housing conditions, poor sanitation and inadequate nutrition were primary contributors to the spread of diseases like TB.
7. *Ibid*, p. 131.
8. Jonathan Bardon, *Belfast, An Illustrated History*, p. 125.
9. Joe Graham, *The Rushlight Magazine*.
10. Jonathan Bardon, *Belfast, An Illustrated History*, p. 220.
11. Uinseann Mac Eoin, *Harry*, p. 31.
12. Taken from a letter from Mary Murray.
13. Michael Farrell, *The Orange State*, p. 152.
14. Uinseann Mac Eoin, *Harry*, p. 73.
15. Uinseann Mac Eoin, *The IRA in the Twilight Years*, 1923–48, p. 519.

16.   Taken from an interview with Madge McConville.

17.   Taken from an interview with Joe Cahill.

18.   Conor Gearty, *The Irish Times*, June 26, 1997.

19.   Taken from an interview with Joe Cahill.

20.   *Ibid.*

21.   *Irish News*, July 29, 1942.

22.   *Ibid*, July 31, 1942.

23.   *Ibid.*

24.   *Ibid.*

25.   Tim Pat Coogan, *The IRA*, p. 234.

26.   Taken from an interview with Joe Cahill.

27.   *The Times*, August 17, 1942.

28.   Tim Pat Coogan, *The IRA*, p. 235.

29.   Steven Moore, *Behind the Garden Wall*, p. 172-73.

30.   *Irish News*, 2nd September, 1942.

31.   *Ibid*, 1st September, 1942.

32.   *Irish Independent*, 31st August, 1942.

33.   *Irish News*, 1st September, 1942.

34.   *Ibid*, 2nd September, 1942.

35.   *Ibid.*

36.   *Ibid.*

37.   *Ibid.*

38.   *News Letter*, 3rd Sept, 1942.

39.   Taken from an interview with Joe Cahill.

40.   *Ibid.*

41.   Uinseann Mac Eoin, *Harry*, p. 100-101.

42.   *Ibid*, p. 130.

43.   *Ibid*, p. 141.

Select Bibliography

Primary Sources

Interviews with Joe Cahill, Madge McConville, Dixie Cordner
and Alfie Hannaway.

Letters from Annie Caldwell, Mary Murray, Joe Cahill, Madge
McConville and Leo Wilson.

Public Record Office, Belfast

Legal Depositions, R. *v* Cordner and Others, 1942.

Crumlin Road Jail records in the cases of Joe Cahill, Jimmy
Perry, Dixie Cordner, Pat Simpson, John Oliver.

Newspapers

Irish News
Belfast Telegraph
Belfast Newsletter
Irish Independent
Irish Times
The Times

Secondary Sources

Bardon, Jonathan, *Belfast: An Illustrated History*, The Blackstaff Press, Belfast, 1982.

—— *A History of Ulster*, The Blackstaff Press, Belfast, 1992

Bowyer Bell, J. *The Secret Army: A History of the IRA*, Dublin, 1970.

Coogan, Tim Pat, *The IRA*, Fontana Books, 1980.

Cronin, Sean, *The McGarrity Papers: Revelations of the Irish Revolutionary Movement in Ireland and America 1900 – 1940*, Anvil Books.

—— *Frank Ryan: The Search for the Republic*, Repsol Publishing / Skellig Press, 1980.

Dernley, Syd with David Newman, *The Hangmans Tale: Memoirs of a Public Executioner*, Pan Books, 1990.

Farrell, Michael *Northern Ireland: The Orange State*, Pluto Press, 1976.

—— *Arming the Protestants: The Formation of the Ulster Special Constabulary and the Royal Ulster Constabulary, 1920 – 27*, Pluto Press, 1983

Graham, Joe, *The Rushlight Magazine*, Belfast

Gray, Tony, *The Lost Years: The Emergency in Ireland, 1939–45*, Warner Books, 1998.

Kelly, James, *Bonfires on the Hillside: An Eyewitness Account of Political Upheaval in Northern Ireland*, Fountain Publishing, 1995.

Kenna, G. B, edited by Tom Donaldson, *Facts and Figures – The Belfast Pogroms, 1920 – 22*, Donaldson Archives, 1997.

Lee, J. J, *Ireland, 1912- 1985: Politics and Society*, Cambridge University Press, 1989.

Mac Eoin, Uinseann. *Harry: The Story of Harry White as Related to Uinseann Mac Eoin, with some Early Photographs, and More Recent Portraits by Colman Doyle*, Argenta Publications, Dublin, 1985.

—— *The IRA in the Twilight Years, 1923 – 48.*

Moore, Steven, *Behind the Garden Wall: A History of Capital Punishment in Belfast*, Greystone Books, 1995.

O'Grada, Cormac, *A Rocky Road: The Irish Economy Since the 1920s*, Manchester University Press, 1997.

Wilson, Leo, *Growing Up in the Hungry, Violent Thirties*, Glandore Publishing, 1997.